LOVING AWARENESS OF GOD'S PRESENCE IN PRAYER

P. FABIO GIARDINI, O.P.

ALBA · HOUSE   NEW · YORK

SOCIETY OF ST. PAUL, 2187 VICTORY BLVD., STATEN ISLAND. NEW YORK 10314

Library of Congress Cataloging in Publication Data

Giardini, Fabio.
    Loving awareness of God's presence in prayer

    Bibliography: p.
    1. GodOmnipresence   2. Prayer.   I. Title.
BT132.G5   231'.4.   78-9654
ISBN 0-8189-0370-8

Imprimi Potest:
Louis Every, O.P.

Nihil Obstat:
Richard T. Adams, M.A.
Censor Librorum

Imprimatur:
Joseph T. O'Keefe
Vicar General, Archdiocese of New York
August 23, 1978

*The Nihil Obstat and Imprimatur are
a declaration that a book or pamphlet is considered
to be free from doctrinal or moral error. It is not implied
that those who have granted the Nihil Obstat and
Imprimatur agree with the contents,
opinions or statements expressed.*

*Designed, printed and bound
in the United States of
America by the Fathers and Brothers of the
Society of St. Paul, 2187 Victory Boulevard,
Staten Island, New York, 10314, as part of their
communications apostolate.*

1 2 3 4 5 6 7 8 9 (Current Printing: first digit).

© *Copyright 1978 by the Society of St. Paul*

(ristampa anastatica)

To my American Sisters, the Dominican Contemplative Nuns, praying that they may always be living witnesses within the Church of an unceasing loving awareness of God's Presence in Prayer.

FOREWORD

"Come to me, all you who are weary and find life burdensome, and I will refresh you" (Mt 11:28). Such is the invitation that Jesus gives to all who would be his followers—an invitation to find in him the meaning of life and the source of lasting joy and peace. It is, in short, an invitation to prayer. And yet, it is an invitation that too frequently goes unanswered.

Jesus has given to every Christian the call to be in relationship with him and with his Father. This call is at the very heart of his teaching: "Father, I pray that they may be one with us" (Jn 17:21). Yet, life today as we know is pervaded by countless elements that seem to thwart a true response to this call. There is the spirit of secularization that upholds productivity and achievement as the sole gauge of personal value and worth. There is the increased busyness of our lives that too often leaves little time for relationship with others and even less with the Lord. There is the secular "virtue" of independence and self-sufficiency that urges us to trust only in ourselves. There is, finally, the lived philosophy that truth resides only in what is tangible and experientially verifiable.

However, even in the midst of these influences there is within more and more people today the awareness of a hunger that can be satisfied only by an encounter with Jesus himself. It is this hunger which Paul describes when he writes that "we ourselves, although we have the Spirit as first fruits groan inwardly while we await the redemption of our bodies" (Rm 8:23). It is this hunger that is moving people today to respond in a fuller way to Jesus' invitation to come to him and the Father in prayer. This renewed interest in prayer is enabling many to recognize the power of the Holy Spirit to transform and give meaning to our lives.

For this reason, Father Giardini's present book on the *Loving Awareness of God's Presence in Prayer* is especially timely. It sets forth, with a sound scriptural basis, a theology of God's presence in the world and then describes how one responds to that presence in prayer. Father Giardini vividly depicts the manifold ways of God's presence throughout salvation history and then presents prayer as a loving response to that presence which opens a person to a continued conversation with God. He further develops a psychology of prayer which shows how prayer enlightens and responds to man's basic existential needs. In this way, he demonstrates that prayer is not an isolated religious event but rather a reality that permeates one's daily life. Father Giardini has offered a unique contribution to Christian circles, for he has grounded prayer not only in a firm biblical tradition but also in an authentic psychology of human experience. He has reminded us that the process of Christian growth entails the total development of the person in loving knowledge and union with God through Jesus Christ and in His Spirit.

I believe that his work will be of genuine service to all who are seeking to understand in a fuller way Jesus' invitation to come to him and the Father in prayer. It should be of special value to those in seminaries, houses of formation, novitiates and colleges who are studying formally the theology of prayer. I am sure it will be for every reader a worthy companion on his journey to the Lord!

† Joseph L. Bernardin
Archbishop of Cincinnati

PREFACE

Prayer is as necessary to Christian life as is breathing to the life of the body. Of course, it is much more necessary and important to actually pray than to know all about what prayer is. However, a better understanding of prayer can more strongly motivate the practice. To grasp *why* (for what purpose) and *how* (in what way) to pray has invariably been a very good way to begin the life of prayer.

One cannot overlook the special relevance prayer has acquired recently. Nowadays, a yearning for prayer is surfacing in many quarters. It finds expression in the emergence of all sorts of new experiments, formal and informal, with respect to both private and communal (devotional and liturgical) prayer. All of this "prayer momentum" seems to be inspired by a new persuasion that the contemplative element is essential to Christian life. But how theologically sound and deep-rooted are the current revivals of prayer? Are we witnessing a mass phenomenon or an elite manifestation? Does this new impulse appear all over the world or is it restricted to certain areas and groups?

The urban technocratic society of our times is pervaded by the spirit of secularism as with a spiritually polluted atmosphere. All "breathing" of authentic prayer seems doomed to be smothered in a social milieu in which

the "death of God" has been proclaimed. It is a matter of
fact that contemporary Christians have serious difficulties in finding convenient times, suitable places and
necessary dispositions for prayer in their secularized daily
living patterns. Nobody denies it! But during the past
decade, quite a few persons have begun to react to this
situation, and have become aware, once again, of God's
presence in their lives. This newly acquired awareness has
greatly vivified their weak prayer lives. Today many
prayer groups act as an enthusiastic vanguard to the
revival of prayer. They function as the leaven in the dough
of our society, but still have a long way to go before
attaining the desired transformation of our present milieu
into a "prayer-fostering" one. At any rate, the myths of an
irreversible march of secularization and of an
irretrievable "death of God" have been dispelled by the
renewed interest in prayer widely found in contemporary
society.

Where affluence and materialism reign, human
persons are hindered in perceiving God's presence,
insofar as everything around them inculcates the
fallacious persuasion that the world of man bears witness
only to man's own achievements and does not proclaim
the glory of God. But despite all the "conspicuous
consumption" those who belong to an affluent society can
afford to display, their basic needs and hunger for
spiritual values and experiences remain utterly un-
satisfied. Today society, hitherto dominated by an
excessive need of materialistic goods, is becoming a
springboard for an authentic search for God's presence in
prayer—for an increasing number of people. When
humans have their "earthly" needs over-satisfied, and
have become literally "fed up" with such a state, their
"heavenly" needs reappear and grow stronger. Beyond
material development and the possession of things, the

eager desire simply to "be" and to "be with God," the supreme loving and beloved Person, enjoys a fresh upsurge of vitality.

Yet the contemporary revival of interest in prayer is not without its dangers and risks. Drawbacks and flaws, faults and aberrations have always lurked in the background of prayerlife throughout the history of Christian spirituality. Errors of the past have received several names, such as hesychasm, illuminism, quietism, sentimentalism, etc. They began with misunderstandings about the role of prayer in Christian salvation and/or with an insufficient integration of prayer into Christian life. The risks of the past are still with us, although they take on a different shape today. Notwithstanding the current and widespread interest in and practice of prayer, a great deal of obscurity and imprecision remain concerning what could be rightly termed the dogmatic foundations of prayer, i.e., the rooting of prayer in God's mystery. Under such circumstances, the danger of sentimentalism comes closer every time prayer is sought for and enjoyed more for its "consoling" power than for its "adoring" value. Such prayer can hardly avoid the danger of becoming only a man-oriented, self-seeking, pleasurable experience, instead of being what it should be: chiefly a God-oriented, self-surrendering and at times crucifying struggle. Sometimes a joyful but shallow spontaneity distinguishes the former type of prayer from the truly contemplative attitude of the spirit, which requires a great deal of painful recollection and detachment. The former type of prayer over-emphasizes human ability—as if man, of his own powers, could enter into intimacy with the Incarnate God and the Indwelling Spirit. It does not take sufficiently into consideration the fact that no authentic experience of divine immediacy can occur apart from the acknowledgement of the utter transcendency of God who abides within a dark cloud of unknowing. And man is absolutely incapable of entering such regions before the Beatific Vision.

Another hazard facing a revival of prayer which may be too swift and too sweeping, is the insufficient integration into the whole of Christian life of the exciting experience enjoyed during the time of prayer. In fact, when the formal prayer session is over, it can happen that little or nothing of its fruits overflow into daily living. And the average praying Christian hardly knows how to bridge the gap between prayer session and daily life. How can he still maintain a spirit of prayer, a contemplative attitude, in his all-too-busy life?

This work hopes to be a sensitive and solid response to the current yearning for prayer—with all its tentative experimentation and possible dangers and hazards. To meet contemporary needs and expectations, a theological work about prayer should follow three major lines of development:

—it must offer a type of prayer which is attainable by every good-willed Christian, so that the spirit of prayer can really permeate daily life through and through;

—it must show how such a spirit of prayer needs to be strongly anchored in God through faith, hope and love of God the Father, who comes to meet us through his Incarnate Son, Jesus Christ, in the Holy Spirit; and

—it must indicate the direction Christian prayer should take: i.e., that when such prayer is not only better understood but thoroughly lived within the total mystery of God made present to man for his salvation, it will also become possible to integrate prayer fully into Christian life. Then will Christian prayer become that all-pervasive attitude taught by our Lord Jesus Christ when he told his disciples that they must pray continuously (Lk 18:1; 21:26; Ep 6:18).

The material in this book was taught to students of spiritual theology both in the United States (at the Catholic University of America) and in Europe (University of Saint Thomas, Rome), and also formed the matter of conferences preached time and again to contemplative and active religious in Europe, the United States and South America, where by God's providence, the author found a broad field of apostolate over the past five years.

Nothing in these pages could have been written without the constant enrichment and corrections afforded by the various audiences that the author has had the honor and joy of addressing. The many persons who asked for this publication and helped in its preparation have all his gratitude. Very special thanks are due to the Dominican cloistered contemplative nuns of the Monastery of the Blessed Sacrament, Farmington Hills, Michigan, who assisted in re-writing the manuscript.

P. Fabio Giardini, O.P.

CONTENTS

PART I

REVELATION AND THEOLOGY
OF GOD'S PRESENCE

INTRODUCTION

"Before the world was made, God chose us in Christ to be holy and spotless, and *to live through love in His presence*" Ep 1:4.

The title of this work, *Loving Awareness of God's Presence in Prayer*, is a short but essential "description of prayer." It is also a general description appropriate for every special form of prayer. Such a description includes two basic elements expressed by the key words *awareness* and *presence*. It points to a union, a *relationship* between the two. Awareness and presence are like the banks of a river, and prayer is the bridge joining one to the other. Or, think of the light which bursts forth from an arc-lamp. Prayer is the light. Man and God are the two negative and positive poles. They cause the light to shine when they are put in the presence of one another.

Awareness

Awareness is a phenomenon which occurs on the side of the praying *human being*. It is the human psychological dimension of prayer. Many psychological acts, attitudes, thoughts, affections and feelings are involved in this word "awareness." Awareness is the "being conscious of" and the "knowing of" a person or thing. An explanation and development of this notion of awareness will be elaborated in detail when we consider the "psychology of prayer."

Loving

The adjective "loving" considered in the Christian context means the actual love of charity (*agape*). Charity is the summit of all Christian life. All virtues which precede charity are prerequisite to charity, and their acts are included in this loving act of prayer. The whole spiritual, natural and supernatural organism of Christian life is put into action through the *loving awareness of prayer*. In a special way, faith and hope, which make up the "theological life" together with charity, are also included. Consequently, this "loving awareness" is also a *believing* and *hoping* awareness. It is an awareness with purity of heart, in humility, in fortitude, and so on. In this loving awareness of prayer all the Christian virtues which charity requires are summed up and offered to God.

Presence

Presence is on the side of God. It is to a "present God" that Christian prayer is addressed. This is the objective, divine-dogmatic dimension of prayer. All divine mystery and its revelation to mankind converge upon and flow into the reality of God's presence. A "theology of prayer" is a reflection on this dimension of prayer.

But what do we mean by "presence"? We can say that it presupposes and includes "existence." But "presence" goes beyond mere existence. "Presence" means "to-be-there-for-someone", not only "to-be" or "to-be-there," as existence alone denotes. God must "be-there-for-us" so that we can address ourselves to him in and through prayer. The mere existence of God, even when accepted in faith, is not sufficient to give birth to prayer.

When God is perceived as present, he is not only believed in as existent in himself. One is also convinced that he leans in mercy and love toward us. He is "felt" as a Person willing and ready to receive us, to listen to us, and to help us lovingly. In other words, it is the presence of God as a loving Person to whom we open up in prayer. Yet, we cannot encounter God as a *loving Person* in prayer unless we open out our hearts to him in an awareness permeated by love of him. We must reciprocate God's loving *presence* with our loving *awareness*. Prayer means a living and loving mutual encounter with and contact between God and us, and us and God. We are mutually present to one another in and through our mutual love.

Our God is the Triune God, and the most perfect presence of God in Christian life is that achieved in the indwelling of the Most Blessed Trinity. Each of the divine Persons has a way of gratifying us with his presence. Each Person manifests his presence in a singular and typical way throughout salvation history. And each Person reveals himself in the personal history of every Christian. Sometimes we may be more sensitive to the presence of one divine Person, and consequently, be more mindful of him in our prayer. There is great multiplicity in God's revelation to man.

Prayer From the Side of God

We intend to begin our consideration of prayer from God's point of view. Both a biblical and a systematic theology of the presence of God will be presented. But an objection could be raised against this approach. One might say that to speak of God and of how he reveals himself as lovingly present to man throughout salvation history is not to speak of prayer. Prayer is an activity of man before God. God does not pray—he does not need to pray at all! It is true that prayer is a human action. There is no prayer in God. The loving awareness of one divine Person to the others is all perfect, but it does not take on the proper character of prayer. For prayer is a need, a hunger aroused and provoked in man by God. It is precisely insofar as man becomes conscious of his creaturely poverty that God appears to him as the only one, infinite, personal Goodness capable of satisfying such hunger. The loving awareness of the presence of God which defines human prayer is absolutely different from the loving awareness without "need or hunger" which the divine Persons enjoy in one another's presence. This distinct presence of the divine Persons to one another within the Blessed Trinity is called "circumincession" in theology.

But the *human* loving awareness of God's presence is a mysterious analogical sharing in the divine, trinitarian loving-awareness, for such divine awareness is the primary source of every other loving awareness man can experience. When this loving awareness is shared by the Holy Trinity with the praying Christian, it is also necessarily conditioned and restricted within the narrow limits of the human creature. This is why a Christian's loving awareness reveals itself as a need and as a response:

As a *need*: i.e., something stirred up by the
                perception of God's goodness;
As a *response*: i.e., a reaction provoked by God
                taking the initiative in
                revealing himself as present
                to man.

Prayer's Responsive Character

When prayer is described as the *dialogue* of man with God, its responsive character is being emphasized. God, by his word, addresses himself to man, and he is always the first to speak. Human prayer is an answer to this divine address. Prayer has been described as the echoing of God's word in our life, or as the reflection of God's light upon our spirit. "You are my Sun, and I am your mirror, O my God!"

The whole of Christian life is a response to God's initiative, his gift of salvation. It is no wonder, then, that prayer—which is the "breathing out" of the same Christian life—follows as a response to the inspiration or "breathing in" of the Holy Spirit who suggests our very words and "groanings" in prayer, as St. Paul teaches.

Against this background of the fundamental human "responsiveness" of the Christian before God, it is quite clear that we must begin our study of Christian prayer with this basic fact or event without which prayer would be impossible. Without this datum, no prayer could be intelligible or reasonable, for the very act of Christian prayer is founded on revelation. Christian prayer presupposes the *full revelation* of God's presence throughout salvation history to all of mankind and to each individual.

Following our study of prayer's responsive character, and its total dependence upon revelation, a theological consideration will help us to put together the many facets of the "presence of God" and to form a clear synthesis on which we can build. We shall then be able to develop a reflection on prayer from the psychological viewpoint. Since God is prior to man, before him and above him, the biblical and theological consideration of the divine presence must precede the study of that human response which actualizes Christian prayer.

The final steps in our research will describe a kind of "psychology of prayer," i.e., a direct approach to prayer as it appears from the side of the praying person, while looking at his own psychology.

Conversation

Prayer can also be defined as a conversation with God. Conversation means dialogue, an encounter in speech, or simply a talk with God. This is a global description which includes both the praying man and God whom he addresses. Such a conversation may have a wide variety of subjects, and may be approached and expressed in different attitudes; petition, demand, adoration, praise, confession of sin or expiation, thanksgiving—each of these "contents" of prayer has a different and characteristic psychological structure. They express man's manifold conditions and states of mind as he perceives God's presence in and through prayer.

Exercise

The following considerations comprise an analysis of

two basic aspects of prayer, for prayer is—at one and the same time—an effort and achievement of man, and a gift or grace from God. Prayer as *exercise* expresses quite precisely this effort on man's part. "Exercise" is required to achieve the loving awareness needed for prayer. Even though a good Christian has the possiblity of becoming lovingly aware of God's presence in prayer, quite often that awareness is inactive. It is "dormant" like some animals in winter. Awareness needs to be stimulated. One needs exercises of recollection, attention and tranquillity, to reach the necessary peace of mind prerequisite to prayer.

On the other hand, awareness in prayer is essentially a *loving awareness*. The love of God, which is Christian charity, requires a previous purification of the heart in order to thrive in a Christian. All other Christian virtues must be practiced to inflame charity—to make it burn, as prayer requires. Consequently, the cultivation of all Christian virtues plus a great deal of recollection and attention is usually needed for satisfying and fruitful prayer. This is the "ascetic" facet of prayer. Self-discipline of body, mind and heart prepare the Christian for encounter with God in prayer's loving awareness.

The ancient Christian writers stressed this ascetical side when they defined prayer as an *ascensus mentis in Deum*, or "the ascent of the mind to God." Prayer, like the climbing of a mountain, is, both psychologically and morally, a laborious, fatiguing endeavor. It is achieved through striving, toilsome and persevering exercise. This is the reason it is often difficult to pray long and well. It is a simple fact that we easily become tired when praying. Prayer becomes a challenge and one is never totally certain of achievement.

Experience

Prayer as an *experience*, on the contrary, implies that God's presence, as one becomes aware of it in the act of praying, is a gift lavished on man. No prayerful attitude can compel God to reveal and grant his presence to man. Now a gift needs to be received by the person benefited in order to be enjoyed or "experienced." Through the reception of God's presence as a gift, the most radical receptivity of man before God is actualized. Therefore, prayer as an experience emphasizes more the offer of God's presence and the infusion of God's gift into the human heart than the actual effort required by man to open his spirit to receive God's presence and gifts. To experience and to enjoy "how good and sweet God is," man must have, over and above everything else, a receptive and docile attitude toward God. This is the reason , from this vantage-point, prayer can better be defined as an *descensus Dei in animam*, "the descent of God into the human soul." Here the man who prays appears as an "enthusiast" (from the Greek word meaning God's taking possession of the human spirit) and a "mystic" who seems able to "touch" the very mystery of God.

Prayer as *experience* and as *exercise* are not only fundamental acts or basic structures in the conversation of man with God. They are also proportioned to the mysterious "position" God keeps in relation to man. The distinction between exercise and experience is founded upon a structurally different way of operating typical of the human psyche. We first turn our gaze and affection toward an object of knowledge and love, which equals "exercise;" and then we stop to grasp and enjoy it, which equals "experience." In prayer, we must also consider the objective ontological position of God in relation to us.

This aspect also gives rise to the twofold operation of soul we call "exercise" and "experience." In fact, God is "present-immanent" and "absent-transcendent" to all creatures, because he is the First and Supreme Cause of their being. But in and through prayer, *man* has a privileged opportunity to realize this position of God present to him in a vivid manner.

Prayer as *exercise*, the "ascent" toward God, clearly implies that God is somehow "up there" or "far" from the usual human manner of living. Properly speaking, the praying man seeks God as the absent-transcendent partner. Prayer as *experience*, the "descent" of God into man, emphasizes God's mysterious intimacy or immanence within man. The praying person can keenly perceive through the above-mentioned structures of prayer that mysterious "presence-in-absence" or "absent-presence" which characterizes God's position toward him or her.

Prayer is essentially a response to God's address and approach to man. The *exercise* of prayer is the human response to the challenge of divine transcendence. The *experience* of prayer is the human response to the gift of divine immanence. Both make up the *conversation* between God and the human person. And this conversation is identical with each entire "transaction" of prayer between God and man.

It is impossible to determine in advance—as if in a "recipe"—the "amount" of human exercise and of human experience required for every prayerful transaction. Both are necessary ingredients, and usually when we try in the exercise of prayer to ascend to God, God himself descends toward us, lavishing upon us his presence in our prayerful experience. Thus, God's free gift and man's free effort encounter one another "half-way," and merge to form the full act of prayer.

The definition of prayer used in the title of this work really means, the "loving awareness of God's presence." Such a definition points to the primary and most evident stage prayerlife reaches when it overcomes the usual absent-mindedness or distraction of man before God. At this stage, to pray means to become lovingly aware of God's presence, since previous to this primary act or attitude of prayer, we are unaware of and practically indifferent to God.

But as the praying person delves more deeply into the loving awareness of God's presence, he or she discovers— with progressively deepening insight—that this is a presence no human loving awareness can comprehend or express. At this stage, prayer can better be described as a "loving-awareness of God's presence-in-absence," or, of "God's transcendent presence." Undoubtedly, God's presence is the "being-there-for-man": the true presence of a loving, caring God, but the one who prays can now perceive so vividly the radical transcendence of God that one's whole prayerlife appears to enter a valley of deep darkness and painful aridity. We seek for a God whom we seem to find surrounded only by a "cloud of unknowing."

The whole process of prayer can thus be divided into three most important stages. The point of departure is the usual human condition of loveless unawareness of God. Prayer simply does not exist at this moment. The first form of prayer results from overcoming that state of non-prayer in a loving awareness of his presence. Eventually, prayer reaches the state of loving-awareness of God's presence-in-absence, or, his transcendent presence. Perhaps an example may help to clarify these three moments in prayer's development.

Imagine a large block of ice breaking off and falling into the sea: an iceberg, which might be seen in summer at the North Pole. At first, the fallen block is almost completely submerged beneath the surface of the water. This may be compared to the stage of human indifference and absentmindedness before God, when all potentialities for loving awareness of his presence remain latent. At the second stage, the block of ice begins to emerge at the sea's surface. This is the time when prayer first appears as loving awareness of the divine presence. But that part of the iceberg which remains underwater is always much larger than what is visible. This is the depth of aridity and darkness before God's transcendence which lies below the surface of any loving awareness of his presence, and which everyone encounters when entering the depths of that first joyful and luminous experience of God in prayer.

Specifically Christian prayer implies and emphasizes two main characteristics: 1) on the one hand, God's presence to men, becoming wonderfully real and personal in and through Jesus Christ in whom the fullness of God dwells "bodily"; and 2), on the other hand, Christians who offer their prayer to God only in and through this same Jesus Christ. Therefore, Christ is the privileged mediator in whom the loving awareness of man and the saving presence of God meet and join in an intimate, interpersonal transaction of prayer.

When we leave this Christian character out of consideration, prayer can still be a religious exercise and experience by means of which one attains peace of mind, knowledge of self, and wisdom of life before God. All religions can meet on a friendly basis and can mutually enrich one another, sharing the fruits of such prayerlife.

But Christian prayer differs *specifically* from every other form of prayer because the "loving awareness of God's presence" implies for the Christian explicit faith in the "bodily," personal presence of God in Jesus Christ. Non-Christian prayer is not conscious of the privileged

mediation of Christ in actualizing the presence of God to
man. God's presence, actualized in and through Christ,
deeply influences and transforms into something essentially different from any kind of non-Christian prayer *all*
the above-mentioned basic forms and structures of
prayer—conversation, exercise and experience.

The *conversation* or dialogue between God and man
which usually takes place in prayer is changed by
Christian faith into an exchange of words which acquire
their full and true meaning only insofar as they converge
upon and are summed up in Our Lord Jesus Christ. He is
the all-meaningful, personified "Word" uttered by God to
man, and the unique "Word" through whom the praying
person's words echo back to God. We stressed above that
prayer is a response to God's *challenge* and to God's *gift*.
This responsive feature of prayer acquires a deeper, more
practical significance when placed against the
background of Christ's death and resurrection. The
exercise of prayer can then become a response to the
challenge of man, represented by Christ's passion and
death; and the *experience* of prayer can transform itself
into a response to Christ's gift to man of the glory of his
resurrection.

The *exercise* of prayer (with all the toil which is
required from the praying person who yearns and strives
to encounter the transcendent God) is for the Christian a
providential opportunity to practice the imitation of
Christ. The Christian achieves some spiritual conformity
with the saving passion and death of his Crucified Lord.
Prayer acquires a sacrificial value through a mysterious,
but real, union with the sacrifice of Christ.

The *experience* of prayer, because of its typical
vividness and joy, assumes within the framework of
Christ's mystery the character of a certain sharing in his
resurrection. In the highest degree of this form of prayer,

this sharing sometimes overflows upon the body of the praying Christian, providing it with a certain similarity to the marvelous condition of the Risen Body of the Lord. Prayer then has a powerful transforming effect upon the Christian, in union and conformity with the resurrection of the Lord.

CHAPTER 1

REVELATION AND REALITY OF GOD'S PRESENCE IN THE OLD TESTAMENT

To understand the theme of God's presence as it is described and developed by the Old Testament, it is useful to keep in mind its essential *structure*, the main *realms* which it permeates, and some of its most typical *features*.

The essential structure as revealed in the Old Testament is made up of the mysterious, immanent-transcendent presence of God. God, by a totally free and loving initiative, reveals his presence in the midst of his people. The people receive the gift of the divine presence in a spiritual way. But usually this divine presence is confirmed and expressed by symbols or material signs. Although the divine presence is made "sensible" to man, it is always perceived, at one and the same time, as an immanent-transcendent, mysterious being and acting of God.

The experience of immanence flows from the fact that God intervenes in the human world, life and history. God is and acts among men. His presence is perfectly suited to man's life, which is a spiritual life in the midst of a material world: in time and space. God is present mainly in and with the people, but He does not disdain to use material, tangible things and places to reach his people and to manifest himself to them.

The experience of transcendence is rooted in the truth that God's presence to man and in the world cannot be contained or encompassed by any human person, thing or place. The God of Israel lavishes his presence on mankind in a wholly free and gratuitous manner. He is not like the pagan gods which cannot help but mingle and identify themselves with elements of the material world, and are "drawn into" man's life and events by compulsory magic words or gestures of human rites.

The main *realms* in which God's presence is manifested to men are cosmic reality and human history. Of course, the word "presence" must be taken in a very broad and analogous sense to fit both realms. Human loving awareness "sees" the divine presence in both realms, even though its "signs" in them are quite different.

Cosmic Presence

A *universal* divine presence permeates the entire material world, and manifests itself to man. It is the *cosmic* presence of God, and it entails the creative omnipotence and omniscience which God exerts upon the whole universe. It can be called "omnipresence" because God acts creatively and governs everything, everywhere, and at the same time in this immense universe.

Examples of this type of presence are often found in the *Psalms* and in the writings of the prophets. "The whole earth is full of his (God's) glory!" (Is 6:3; Nb 14:30) "Can anyone hide in a dark corner without my seeing him? It is Yahweh who speaks; do I not fill both heaven and earth?" (Jr 23:24) "Where could I go to escape your

(God's) spirit? If I climb the heavens, you are there; if I lie in Sheol, you are there too. . ." (Ps 139:7-8). A dreadful manifestation of God's powerful presence is perceived by the praying person in earthquakes, storms, volcanoes (Ps 29:3-6; 97:1-6), because all of these things are creatures of God which obey his commands.

All material creatures can be summoned by the one who prays to sing God's praises before his presence. "Let the heavens be glad; let earth rejoice, let the sea thunder and all that it holds; let all the woodland trees cry out for joy at the presence of Yahweh, for he comes. . ." (Ps 96:11-13). Also, the well-known hymn of the three young men in the fiery furnace calls upon "all things the Lord has made to bless the Lord, to give glory, and eternally to praise him" (Dn 3:52ff). Needless to say, this universal-cosmic presence of God is founded upon the divine and ongoing act of creation and government of the entire world.

Another *special* presence of God in the Old Testament is found in God's revelation and in salvation history. It can be qualified as *historical* because it is characterized by local and temporal relations. In fact, this is a presence of God which occurs in particular *places* where it seems in some way "localized," although it cannot be bound to that place. It is as it appears in particular *moments* of Israel's history, and is shown by several typical "signs" (as the cloud, the pillar of fire, the tent or tabernacle and other signs). Referring to the most significant of these signs, the tabernacle, some exegetes call it the "tabernacling presence of Yahweh." All of salvation history can be summed up in this loving and saving historical presence of God to his chosen people. Therefore, we are more interested in it than the cosmic presence, previously mentioned.

This distinction between the cosmic and the tabernacling presence of Yahweh can be useful for a better

understanding of our topic. However, the two forms of
presence should not be dichotomized; they are simply two
ways of manifesting the unique presence of God to man.
The one same God is Creator of the universe and Savior
of the world. God's creation and governance of the
universe are conceived by the Old Testament as the first
act in the entire drama of salvation. Consequently, the
divine presence founded on creation is only a basic form
of presence presupposed and completed by the presence
established in the midst of Israel by the divine work of
salvation.

The most important *features* of the biblical theme of
God's presence are two: 1) At every period of salvation
history, this theme appears as so all-embracing and
central that the history of God's relations with his
creatures, and especially with the people of Israel, is none
other than the history of his ever loving and saving
presence in their midst. Such history is, up to a point, co-
extensive with that of humanity itself, and we may even
say with that of the whole universe. The theme of God's
presence is all-pervading and *radical*. It is interiorly
linked with and permeates all other themes of the *Bible*:
e.g., revelation, salvation, reconciliation, re-capitulation.
2) From the viewpoint of salvation history as a whole, the
theme of God's presence has a clearly *progressive*
character. It is ever developing from a little primal seed
toward its fullest blossoming and fructification. It is still
going through various stages of unfolding or evolution in
our time—beyond the written *Bible*—and will continue to
develop until the Parousia. While it passes from one stage
to the next, it grows. It becomes more explicit and more
profound; it achieves an ever higher degree of clarity and
inwardness. In fact, the divine presence moves from
things to persons, from fleeting moments to enduring
persistence, from the performance of divine actions to the

sharing of God's gifts and graces, always aiming at that final peak-event when God will be altogether openly and inwardly "all-in-all." This theme is so complex that any attempt to trace in it a rigid succession of stages can hardly succeed. However, for the sake of clarity, we will follow the successive eras of biblical history, even though our distinctions should not be taken as absolutely clear-cut or exclusive divisions.

Primordial History

In the primordial story of creation and sin in the terrestrial paradise, we can already find the original distinction between the two forms of presence mentioned above. All creatures are called into existence by the all-powerful and all-knowing "Word" of God. This fact implies that God is always present to his creatures through his omniscience and omnipotence. Man is called into being by a very special act of God's creative power. Man has received the breath of life from God himself, who "breathed into man's nostrils," and so, somehow shared his own divine life and power with man. It is for this reason that the human person bears in himself a "functional" image of and likeness to his Creator: as Lord of the universe. Consequently, man's closeness to God and God's presence to him are particularly intimate, and are reserved to man alone among all visible creatures.

However, the word "likeness" (of man to God) excludes the idea of equality. It also weakens the force of the word "image" which is a realistic term (literally, "something carved") implying a physical resemblance, such as that between Adam and his son (Gn 5:3). But man's special relation to God marks him off from the animals. It involves a general similarity of nature and activity with God: man is a person, has intellect, will and especially, authority over other creatures in a way similar to God. Therefore, man can have a mutual personal presence with God, and this intimacy is described as God "walking in the garden" to converse with Adam, as a friend paying a visit to his friend. Though this description is pure anthropomorphism it succeeds wonderfully well in giving a lively sense of the presence of God on earth, and keeps the idea of that presence to man real and vivid.

Unfortunately, this intimate presence of God to man is soon interrupted by sin, i.e., by disobedience to God. The break is so extensive that after sin, man becomes ashamed and afraid to meet his God. He goes to hide himself among the bushes of the garden. Thenceforth God and man are unable to encounter one another in a friendly way. Instead, God changes into a severe judge who punishes man's fault, and banishes him from the garden, where he had enjoyed the divine presence and friendship. The primordial story interprets our actual current situation before God and teaches us that the original friendly presence and intimacy willed by God for us has been tragically destroyed by man's disobedience. Needless to say, man cannot enjoy God's presence when he acts against the divine will as a sinner. Because we live far from God's presence, suffering and toil, sweat and pain, come upon us, and keep us "outside of paradise." It is no longer easy or enjoyable for us sinners to dwell in God's presence. Rather, as sinners, we are afraid and ashamed before God whom we face as our judge, and no longer as a friend. The history of salvation recorded throughout the Bible reflects the progressive re-establishment of the divine loving-presence in our midst.

The Time of the Patriarchs

God's presence in *the time of the patriarchs* is manifested through his frequent apparitions to them, and through his interventions in their lives. The *events and setting* of God's self-revelation always have a similar basic structure. God is the first to take the initiative in appearing and addressing himself to the patriarchs. He reveals his will to them, and promises them his assistance, provided they accept his will and follow it. God comes to encounter them in their nomadic wanderings and wherever they pitch their tents. Because of his apparition, some places become privileged situations for communication with him. To respond to God's revelation and to mark off the places where he appeared, the patriarchs erected a stele or built an altar. There they prayed and offered sacrifices, worshipping God there in a special way, acknowledging the greatness and mercy of their God.

The patriarchs' experience of God's revelation and presence show some *typical traits*. Sometimes the apparition arouses a vivid sense of consolation in them: their response to God's nearness and his care of them (Gn 28:10-22). At other times, they experience his presence as toilsome and painful. Such is the patriarch's response to God's challenge and demands (Gn 32:23-31). This twofold, almost contradictory experience, is a sign of the mysterious immanence-transcendence of God in relation to man. However comforting or challenging, God's presence, experienced by the patriarchs, is always *fleeting*. God has not yet a stable and unique dwelling-place on earth. Sometimes he appears in one place, sometimes in another. His presence to man is still like the presence of a "passing guest" (Gn 18).

Moses and the Exodus

With respect to God's presence in *the time of Moses and during the Exodus*, let us consider the setting: the human experience of it; and its realization. Moses is introduced as the heir of the ancient patriarchs, for their personal, direct revelation and experience of God's presence is renewed in his life (the Burning Bush on Mt. Sinai, Ex 3). Since he is the great leader and lawgiver of Israel, Moses has an exceptionally intimate experience of the presence of God: the living and loving God reveals his *will of liberation* for the people of Israel through his speaker, Moses. This will of God, expressed in the Law of the Covenant, constitutes Israel as "the People of God": the elected people within whom God dwells by His demanding and protecting presence. Moses is solemnly appointed to act as *mediator* between God and his people. God's will and presence are revealed to the people only in and through his servant, Moses. The manifestation and experience of the presence of God to Moses occurs especially at two times and places: on *Mount Sinai*, the "mountain of God," he appears, manifesting his powerful and terrible presence by fire, thunder, and earthquakes. Here God gives to Moses the "Law of the Covenant" for his people, Israel. In the *Desert*, God reveals his caring and loving presence in "the cloud" by day, and the "pillar of fire" by night. Here Moses goes to visit him and converse with him at the "tent of meeting."

Each of the many signs and symbols of the divine presence which are emphasized during the wanderings of the people through the desert have a special significance. The *Cloud* wonderfully symbolizes both God's transcendence and immanence. The cloud is an element of heaven, where God lives (= transcendence), and it comes down from heaven to dwell in the midst of the people. (=

immanence). So, the cloud reveals God's presence, but it also veils the divine nature from human eyes, just as the "cloud of unknowing" in which God draws nearer to men while hiding himself. The "dark night" (*noche obscura*) of the Spanish mystics is akin to this biblical "cloud."

The *glory* is frequently connected with the cloud. Even more than the cloud, it is identified with God himself. The Hebrew word *kabod* suggests the idea of "weight," taken as a symbol of God's omnipotence. God reveals His presence through His might. The Greek word *doxa*—used by the Septuagint to translate the Hebrew *kabod*—expresses the idea of dazzling splendor and an unapproachable light. It does not contradict the darkness implied in the word "cloud": too much light is experienced as darkness.

Undoubtedly, *kabod* and *doxa* point out that the "divine glory" is beyond any human possibility of grasping or experiencing. The reality of God's transcendence is therefore implied in the very words used to express the divine manner in which he reveals himself to man. However, those words really point to God's presence (or immanence) in the midst of his people. As a matter of fact, they are frequently used as synonyms for the Aramaic word *shekinah*, which directly means the divine indwelling. Because of its sound, the word *shekinah* was also connected with the Greek word *skene*, which means "tent." Indeed, another important sign of God's presence in the midst of his people is the "tent of meeting" or the "rendezvous" between God and his people through the mediation of Moses who entered the tent to speak with God "face to face" as to a friend, according to the Elohist tradition. The same tent or tabernacle also contained the *ark* of the covenant. It was called the "tent of testimony," according to the priestly tradition. By the ark, which contained the tablets of the

Law, God made known his will. The divine will, of course, was practically identified with the very Person of God. Hence, it was believed that God was dwelling within the ark, and standing over the tent or tabernacle—and from there guiding and protecting his people through Moses, his speaker. Notwithstanding this materialization of God's presence, the transcendence of God was always respected. Constructed in accordance with the model preconceived in heaven, the tabernacle (like the temple after it) was a kind of image or copy of God's temple in heaven, wherein the transcendent God dwells and abides in the full sense of the words.

As far as man's experience of God's presence is concerned, we find in *Exodus* a confirmation of what was revealed to the patriarchs—with some relevant perfecting of it, though it is still quite limited. In *Exodus* the revelation of God's presence occurs through material things and phenomena, just as in the time of the patriarchs. The material signs, which simultaneously make known and hide the presence of God in respect to men, keep emphasizing the paradoxical, mysterious position of God: immanence and transcendence, a presence-in-absence, a presence of God "localized," but without being bound to any particular place or object, because God reveals himself and acts *everywhere*: God is omnipotent and omnipresent.

Some progress in the revelation of the divine presence can be noted in *Exodus*. There is a clear improvement in the *duration* of his presence in the midst of men. The typical fleetingness of God's apparitions to the patriarchs has been succeeded by the permanence of his saving presence among his people in the desert. "I will dwell in the midst of the Israelites and be their God; they shall know me for the Lord God that rescued them from the land of Egypt, to abide among them, as their Lord and their God" (Ex 29:45-46; Lv 26:11-12, ff). But this new divine presence does not yet have perfect permanence. The "cloud" will cease to escort the people when it reaches the Promised Land, and the tabernacle will then be replaced by the temple. With an improvement in duration, we also have in *Exodus* a deepening of the human understanding of God's presence. It becomes quite clear at this point that God does not dwell, properly speaking, in any particular place or thing. But rather, he abides with and among his people, so that where his people are, Yahweh also is present.

Let us call this the *socio-historical* presence of God; a presence brought about by God within the social group He has elected—the people of Israel, living on earth and throughout various historical events. In itself, this form of divine presence is neither local nor temporal. Yet it becomes, to some extent, both local and historical insofar as the people of Israel, whom God has chosen for his special abode on earth, lives in a given place and time. Because God wants to encounter his people through events, he reveals his presence in time and place, when and where the people are. The cloud, the pillar of fire, the tablets of the Law, and the tent are only tangible signs of a deeper presence of God brought about by his saving, caring, and demanding Word-Will revealed to his people. God makes himself present to his people as their Lord and Leader. Through his guidance and commands, he is present to the group which accepts him as their God. He is present, then, where he makes known his *Will* and carries it out. He is in the midst of his people and with them to fulfill his plan to save them from Egypt and to lead them into the Promised Land.

The means and manner of realizing God's presence are, in *Exodus*, particularly new and important. But this newness is not primarily represented by the signs through which the divine presence is revealed, even though these are more numerous and more typical than those in the time of the patriarchs, i.e., the cloud, the pillar of fire, the ark and other signs. The most specific and important newness is found in the *mediation of Moses*, through whom God makes himself especially accessible, present and active to and for his people. The presence God establishes among his people is, as said above, his divine saving Word-Will. It is God's Law and Covenant abiding within an obedient and worshipping community. But Moses is the only one who can encounter, "see," and speak to God "face to face" (Dt 34:10; Nm 12:1-8). By his own inner experience of God's will, Moses knows what are God's wishes and what commandments are to be kept by his people. Moses alone is such a friend of God that he can intercede, obtain forgiveness, obtain water, manna and other needs of the people. All of Israel's relations with its God and God's presence to Israel are carried out through the mediation of Moses. Such actualization of the divine presence among men is at first granted only to an individual. But such intimacy with him is later extended and shared with others. This seems to be a common pattern of salvation history. In *Exodus*, the pattern reaches its full expression in Moses himself—and thus foreshadows the Person and mission of Christ. Nevertheless, this divine presence actualized through Moses' mediation is still imperfect. The God made present through his prophet in the midst of Israel is chiefly a Lawgiver and Ruler, to whom the people must respond mainly with an attitude of fearful obedience. Such "authoritarianism" seems to demand more of an exterior than an inner submission to the divine presence. Moreover, it is not each individual who personally receives this gift. The people as a group receive the Law and God's Will and his presence associated with it. Since the divine presence abides within the people as such, the entire nation is "consecrated" to God, and individual members did not seem to need any inner moral sanctity. God's presence is not conceived of as indwelling and as sanctifying each person in his intimate "heart" and life. It is only a presence which guides the people and strengthens them in the collective implementation of God's will to liberate Israel from Egyptian slavery and lead it out to the conquest of the Promised Land.

David and Solomon

A further decisive step for the actualization of God's presence among his people is made in the *time of David and Solomon* (c. 1000 B.C.). After the death of Moses, the so-called "Judges" took over his mission with authority as charismatic military chiefs for Israel's total conquest of Palestine. They were possessed by the "Spirit of God," which gave them the courage to achieve great military exploits, but without transforming their inner lives. As a matter of fact, they do not appear as very devout in the sense of having a genuine experience of God's presence. They even seem to exhibit little concern for God himself.

The ark, symbol of the Covenant between God and his people, and the center of the divine presence in Israel during all this time, remained in Bethel. Once it was captured by the Philistines, but they hastened to return it to the Israelites due to the troubles and disasters it caused among them. The worship of God was practised in various places, as in Masphat, Ramatha, Gilgal and other places.

King David represents a turning-point in the historical evolution of Israel. It was he who made plans for making the city of Jerusalem the chief sacred City of

God. Near to his kingly palace, a temple in honor of
Yahweh was to be built, and the ark would be transferred
there. David did not live to bring about his project, and it
remained for his son, Solomon, to be the actual builder of
Jerusalem's temple.

The significance of David's project was both *political
and religious*. David was one of the greatest political
figures of Israel's history. He understood that after
capturing Jerusalem, and being left as its only king, he
had a good opportunity for bringing political unity to the
divided tribes. Now, the strongest bond of unity linking
the Israelites together was the fact of having the same
religion of Yahweh, a religion which the tribes had kept
since the time of the Exodus. Therefore, David realized
that he could found the political unity of the whole people
of Israel upon its religious unity, so that both forms of
unity would support and sustain one another.

To implement this project, he placed the capital of his
kingdom in Jerusalem. There, near to his royal palace, he
planned to transfer the ark, symbol of God's presence
among the people. He planned to build there a
magnificent temple to Yahweh. In this way everyone
could easily make the connection between religious and
political power, and between religious and political unity.
Since the king's palace was near the dwelling-place of
Yahweh, so too, the authority of the king would somehow
result from and be united with the divine Power of
Yahweh over his people. By means of this proximity, both
the prestige of the king and the cohesion of the people
would be "consecrated" by God's presence.

It would certainly be incomplete and false to think
that such a deeply religious man as David wanted to use
the religious unity of the people and the omnipotence of
Yahweh only to uphold the political unity of his kingdom
and his power over it. The religious motivation of David

in projecting the construction of God's temple was, undoubtedly, paramount, all-inclusive, and absolutely pure. David wanted to show his gratitude to Yahweh who had protected him from many dangers, and who had established him King of Israel. David wanted to submit, and offer his kingship to Yahweh, his God. In this way, Jerusalem became at once the "city of David" and the "city of Yahweh," or simply, "Yahweh-is-there," (Ezk 48:35), the city of the "being-thereness-of-God." Consequently, David's project had the chief effect of renewing the strict association between the political history of Israel and the salvation history of Yahweh, while all is permeated by a more localized and centralized presence of God abiding in a unique dwelling-place, right in the midst of his people. The time of nomadic wandering through the desert is now definitely over for Israel. Yahweh no longer dwells in a tent or tabernacle, in a "wanderer's house," when present to his people. From now on, he will dwell in a "settler's house" as does Israel herself, in a temple as splendid as the palace in which the king lives.

God fully accepts David's project, but gives it a deeper meaning and a greater extension and relevance in the history of salvation. The answer of Yahweh to David's proposal is contained in Nathan's prophecy (cf. 2 S 7:5-16; 1 Par 17). In short, Yahweh says: "You, David, intend to build a house of stone for my dwelling-place in Jerusalem, but I, Yahweh, abide among men and not in a place. Therefore, I will abide among my people mainly through you and your royal dynasty, which will remain unshaken forever." The *Bible* plays on words when it expresses these ideas. David offers God a "house of stone" to live in. God accepts the offer, and responds by promising to establish through David a "royal house" (in the sense of lineage) over his people. Yahweh says, "It is not you, David, who will provide me with a house. I, Yahweh, will change you and your descendants into a royal house which will reign over my people forever." In such a prophetic answer to David the following is proclaimed:

—the generosity of God: he gives much more than he receives.
—the essentially "human" character of Israel's religion: for Yahweh is neither directly concerned with nor bound to places and material things. Rather, he abides among his people through human beings elected to be his mediators.
—the beginning of the messianic promise of God: this will be fully achieved in Jesus Christ, the "Son of David."

We find here a clear formulation of that "royal messianism" which is typical of Israel. Her later history will be changed by this prophecy into a constant expectation of a Savior-King, who shall restore and fulfill the kingdom of David. David is the first anointed king or "Messiah" who will attain through Jesus Christ, after many centuries, the fulfillment of God's promise made to his "house," (Lk 1:32-33). Notice the similarity between Nathan's prophecy and the words of Luke. From this time on, God's presence among his people "localized" in the temple of Jerusalem, and God's support of the house of David, reigning over Israel, will always be bound together. Even when the Davidic monarchy was deprived of the kingdom and the temple was destroyed, God's promise of a messianic kingdom retained its full strength and value.

The actual building of the temple in the time of Solomon is a typical example of a gratuitous divine action in response to a human offering. The construction of the temple brings about an historical project. It is not the realization of a cosmic myth, as it usually was for the temples of the pagans surrounding Israel. The temple of Jerusalem is devoutly dedicated to Yahweh. It does not represent a sort of pressure exerted upon the divinity through the use of magic rites, performed at the founding of pagan temples. The heathens thought that their divinities were identified with cosmic forces; that they could be compelled to dwell within the temples built for them by means of the rites of dedication. Yahweh is the Creator and Lord of the world, infinitely superior to any natural forces, and therefore cannot be compelled by men to dwell anywhere. He is absolutely free before the offer of a temple as his dwelling-place. This freedom distinguishes the transcendence of Yahweh from the cosmic, exclusively "immanent" gods of the heathen.

Due to Yahweh's free predilection for David, Solomon, and the people of Israel, he is willing to consecrate with his special presence the temple built for him. Eventually, Yahweh's constant presence in the temple turns into one of his most precious gifts to his people. Beginning with the time of Solomon, the entire historical and religious life of Israel develops and flourishes around the divine presence in Jerusalem's temple. From the temple Yahweh reigns over his people and shows them his concern and love. The fidelity of the people is measured in relation to the worship performed in the temple before Yahweh's presence. The temple represents above all the solemn institutionalization of the "material," tangible dimension of God's presence among his people. We have already noted that throughout the *Bible*, the presence of God is quite often associated with and symbolized by material things and places. Without doubt, Yahweh has an absolutely immaterial nature. Man is corporeal; he is a bodily being surrounded by material things, and he lives in time and space. He needs, therefore, to encounter God in places and through materialities— the only symbols of the divine transcendent presence which are proportionate to man's nature.

Such institutionalization of the "material" aspect of God's presence among his people represents a remote foreshadowing of the bodily, personal presence of God in Jesus Christ. Indeed, Christ spoke of his body as the true temple of God, "wherein dwells the fullness of the deity." Moreover, Jesus Christ is the heir of David, whose dynasty built the temple as the dwelling-place of God. Consequently, the meaning of the temple and the promise of God to David on the occasion of its being built will both find in Jesus, the true Messiah and Incarnate Son of God, their full accomplishment.

Mission of the Prophets

As far as our topic is concerned, *the Prophets' mission* seems to have been chiefly that of preventing the people of Israel from remaining fixed in the institutionalization of God's presence which, from the time of Solomon, was "localized" in the temple of Jerusalem.

The impressive, solemn liturgy of the temple exposed Israel constantly to the temptation of thinking that God's presence among his people was perfectly and finally achieved in Jerusalem's temple. In their fight against this danger, the prophets struggled to overcome any sort of ritualistic and religious conservatism, and to uproot any false trust in the security supposedly found in the cult and traditions of Israel. At the same time, however, they developed a deeper experience of and teaching on the divine presence. Their teaching strongly emphasizes, as never before in the Old Testament, some of the dialectic tensions emerging from the complexity of God's presence:

—The tension between immanence and transcendence, or presence and absence: God dwells on earth in his temple, but his only appropriate dwelling-place is in heaven.
—The tension between God's special and universal presence on earth: God is particularly present in the midst of his people, but his power extends to all kingdoms and nations of the world.
—The tension between God's ritual or "tabernacling" presence, and the moral or spiritual presence within Israel: God is especially present within the temple where constant worship is offered to him, but he establishes his spiritual presence also in the life of those who do his will.

The first and second tensions have little novelty in the teaching of the prophets. But the third is so typical and relevant to their teaching that at times it seems to be their main point. The prophets fully recognize and accept that the temple of Jerusalem is the dwelling-place of Yahweh (Is 6; Jr 7:10-11). But they stress God's closeness to his people in loving kindness, developing considerably the revelation of his caring, passionate, tender "wedded love" for them. "I, (Yahweh) will betroth you to myself forever, betroth you with integrity and justice, with tenderness and love. I will betroth you with faithfulness, and you will come to know Yahweh. . ." (Ho 2:21; Jr 2:2-7; 3:6-8).

In the line of the dialectical tension arising in their writings between the "tabernacling" or ritual and the "wedded love" or spiritual presence of God, the prophets work out a more developed doctrine of the human response to the divine presence. Actually, they point to two different but complementary ways in which man responds to God. There is the response given by the people through the observance of the *ritual* precepts of the divine law. Such a response is realized by the solemn, public liturgy offered daily to Yahweh in his dwelling-place on earth, the temple. And there is also that response which consists in the observance of the *moral* commandments of the Law. Such a response demands the practice of personal righteousness, social justice, and love for one's neighbor, especially for the needy and the poor, for "orphans and widows." The prophets are strongly convinced and consistently preach that both religious responses are required by God as a counterpart to keeping his protective presence among the Israelite people. They proclaim the absolute ritual primacy of God's presence in Jerusalem's temple, rejecting any sort of idolatry. They also stress the total nonexistence and impotence of pagan deities, their "nothingness," and they remind the people of the worthlessness and impiety which idol-worship brings about (Ho 2:7-15; Jr 2:3-15).

But the prophets are not content with the mere ritual observance offered to God in the temple. Their characteristic dissatisfaction with a worship limited to external gestures leads them to condemn resolutely any sin or moral transgression of the Law—because such behavior takes away God's presence from the people. Over and over again, they call for an inner and socially effective virtuous life. They believe that this is absolutely necessary if the saving presence of God is to be preserved in the temple as well as in the very midst of the daily life of the people.

Sins or transgressions of the moral precepts, no less than idolatry or transgressions of the ritual law, cut the people off from God's presence. "Your iniquities have made a gulf between you and your God. Your sins have made him veil his face so as not to hear you" (Is 59:2). Transgressions of the moral Law are considered by the prophets as opposition to Yahweh, who is the "God of Justice" (Amos), the "God of Love" (Hosea), the "God of Holiness" (Isaiah). Jeremiah "sees" sin as a collective evil which infects the whole nation, and it calls for a dreadful judgment in "the day of Yahweh." But he also speaks of the individual moral responsibility and of punishment proportionate to individual guilt (Jr 31:20-30, which will later be developed in Ezk 18 and 33:10-20). The prophets emphasize the people's need of a genuine search for God, which includes the inner conversion of the heart from sin and the exterior exercise of social justice.

The sins committed against the moral law are, in the opinion of the prophets, so devastating in removing God's presence from the people that they often protest vehemently against any public worship not associated with righteous moral conduct. Such mere ritual righteousness falsely infuses into the people the presumptuous and "magic" security of being protected by God's presence! Therefore, it is abominable to Yahweh and to the prophets.

Taking into account all the prophetic condemnations of the temple and its worship, some Protestant exegetes have exaggerated the opposition of the prophets to the ritual of Israel's religion. This is incorrect because the prophets neither deny the great religious value of public worship, nor reject God's "tabernacling presence" in the temple. Rather, they spur Israel to strive for the integration between ritual religion expressed in worship, and moral religion proved by conduct. They repeatedly exhort that worship and the practice of the moral virtues be united, since both are equally required and pleasing to Yahweh (Is 1:11-17; Jr 6:20; Ho 6:6-8).

We can say that between worship related to the

"tabernacling presence" of God and moral life, there is in the prophets no opposition, but rather mutual complementarity. This vivid and manifold appreciation of God's presence is intimately related to their personal experience. Indeed, the prophets enjoyed a direct "mystical" contact with God, who communicated to them his "Word" and gave them the task of passing it on to others—thus making everyone able, to some extent, to share in their own experience of God. The prophets were great witnesses to this highly precious and mysterious presence of God who speaks, through his divine Word, within man's spirit, and gives meaning and value to all human life and history.

CHAPTER 2

GOD'S PRESENCE
THROUGH JESUS CHRIST
IN THE NEW TESTAMENT

The doctrine of God's presence (in constant development throughout the Old Testament) has been abundantly harvested as a ripe fruit in the New. We must be content here with only a sketchy and systematic presentation of the most important elements which compose that doctrine, in the hope of completing our survey of the *Bible*. We have, especially in the New Testament, the living source of Christian prayer—the loving awareness of God's presence actualized in us through Jesus Christ.

God-With-Us

Before his birth, Christ was announced as *"God-with-us" (Emmanuel)*. In the uniqueness of himself, Jesus Christ sums up all the forms of God's presence to man revealed and established in the Old Testament. The divine presence in Christ is like the summit of a pyramid: all other forms found throughout the Old Testament reach their perfect unity and accomplishment in him.

God's presence in the ark, the tabernacle, the temple of Jerusalem, the so-called "tabernacling presence," which was in the Old Testament a "localized" and "material" form of the divine presence, is brought to its fulfillment at the Incarnation of the Son of God in Jesus Christ. "The Word became flesh and 'pitched his tent' among us, full of grace and glory; we have beheld His glory, the glory of an only Son coming from the Father" (Jn 1:14). The glory of God hovering over the ancient tabernacle forms the background of this passage. In an even clearer manner, Christ's body is called the new "temple of God, not made by human hands" (Mk 14:58). In short, Jesus Christ is the most privileged "place" of God's tabernacling presence among men. "For in him the whole fullness of deity dwells bodily" (Col 2:9). Christ is the most perfect embodiment of the "tabernacling presence" of Yahweh.

After Christ's death and resurrection, this presence of God in him will attain its eternal status in the heavenly city where there will be no temple, "for its temple is the Lord God Almighty and the Lamb. And the city has no need of sun or moon to shine upon it, for the glory of God is its light, and its lamp is the *Lamb*" (Rv 21:22-23). The Lamb is Jesus Christ, the Lamb of God who takes away the sin of the world.

On the other hand, God's presence is constantly renewed on earth by the *Eucharist*, since "the cup of blessing which we bless is a communion with the blood of Christ" (1Co 10:16-17). The celebration of the Eucharist is therefore the center of all Christian liturgy and prayer, the main rite through which the Christian intimately encounters and fully worships God's "tabernacling" presence in and through Jesus Christ.

God's *"personal presence"* in the many figures of the Old Testament who shared in different ways and degrees

Of God's Presence in Prayer

in the living, guiding, saving care of God for his people is preeminently and wholly actualized in Our Lord Jesus Christ. Within this "personal" presence, we can distinguish a "representative" and a "spiritual" form. The patriarchs, the priests, the prophets, the kings, were all religious leaders of Israel who shared differently in the manifold "*representative*" presence of Yahweh among his people. Because he takes the position of a unique Mediator between God and man, Christ Jesus sums up in himself the prophetic, kingly and priestly "representative" presence of God. Jesus assumes into the unity of his mysterious Person and saving mission, at one and the same time, the roles of Prophet, King, and Priest usually exercised by different persons in the Old Testament. Therefore, Jesus possesses the fullness of the manifold representative presence used by God in the Old Testament. The "*spiritual*" presence of God among his people was the special benevolence and protection Yahweh showed to the pious Israelites who obeyed not only the ritual but also the moral precepts of the Law with great humility, trust, and self-surrender to Yahweh:the "anawim" or "poor of Yahweh." As far as the benevolent presence of God is concerned, Jesus Christ identifies himself with these "poor." "As you did it to one of the least of my brethren, you did it to me" (Mt 25:31-46). Moreover, he appears as the perfect personification of the "Suffering Servant" foretold by Isaiah; the One in whom God's presence through his will and man's docile acceptance of it merge into each other. "My Father, if it be possible, let this cup (of death) pass me by. Nevertheless, let it be as you, not I, would have it" (Mt. 26:39).

The previous few hints show quite clearly that the whole revelation and actualization of God's presence among his people eventually reaches its climax in Jesus Christ. In him it attains its most synthetic form and its full

flowering or perfection. Jesus Christ is "God-with-us" par
excellence; he "Who reflects the glory of God and bears
the very stamp of his nature, upholding the universe by his
word of power" (Heb 1:3). The whole mystery of God's
presence to man is fully concentrated in and marvelously
manifested in the very Person of Jesus Christ. Those who
believe in Jesus as their Savior and Lord cannot have any
awareness of God's presence in prayer except through
Jesus Christ and in union with him.

Man's Participation in Christ

Jesus did not reserve to himself the full possession of
God's presence that he enjoyed. He came to call all men to
believe in him, and thus, through him, to get in touch with
the most perfect and highest form of the divine presence
actualized in a human being. He also offered all believers
the grace of union with him. In him, Christians share in
the same divine presence which the Person of Christ
possesses fully.

Thus a real joining-with and an actual sharing-in
occurs for both individual Christians (the "faithful") and
for the Christian community (the "Church"). Both
occurrences have a specific and decisive relevance for
Christian prayer. The awareness of God's presence which
brings about the act of prayer can be aroused and
nourished in a Christian by his encounter—through faith
and love—with the individual Christian and with the
whole Church. This happens insofar as both have some
participation in God's presence perfectly established in
Christ.

As far as the participation of the *individual Christian*
in all forms of God's presence actualized in Christ is
concerned, the complex teaching of the New Testament

requires us to distinguish and to arrange in synthetic order:

—the main *means*;
—the most important *aspects*;
—the final earthly *accomplishment* of that participation.

Faith and *baptism* are, according to the New Testament, the *main means* that the Christian has at his disposal for encountering Christ and being united with him.

Faith presupposes and includes the religious "about-face" performed through conversion, wherein many typical Christian virtues such as repentance, confession of sins, humility, and trust in the saving power of God are involved. The positive spiritual movement of conversion in its tending toward the very Person of Christ merges with and turns into faith, or better still, into a "believing in" him. Through that total self-surrender or adhesion of mind, heart and behavior to Jesus Christ, expressed by the meaningful "believing in," the Christian acknowledges him as the unique One who brings to mankind God's saving presence in its most perfect form. Christians believe that Jesus is "the Son of God who came into this world" (Jn 11:17; Rm 10:9); that Jesus Christ and God the Father "are one" (Jn 10:30; 17:21); that "Jesus is in the Father and the Father is in him," so that "he who has seen him has seen the Father," who in and through Jesus preaches the Good News and performs the work of salvation (Jn 14:9-11; 12:44; 14:1).

By faith, the Christian attains the vision of "the Truth," of "the Light," which is Jesus Christ (Jn 3:19-21; 12:35-36, 46), so that he may walk in the light as the people of Israel followed the "pillar of fire" through the desert—symbol and evidence of the caring, saving presence of God among them (Jn 8:12).

True faith sums up both the human search for and the attainment of God's presence in Jesus Christ. Consequently, to believe, especially according to St. John, means to enter into the sphere of divine life and presence enjoyed to the utmost degree by Jesus Christ. So true is this that the faithful receive "power of becoming children of God," as Jesus Christ in whom they abide is "the only Son from the Father" (Jn 1:9-14). "No one who denies the Son has the Father. He who confesses the Son has the Father also. . .If what you heard from the beginning (namely, that Jesus Christ is the only Son of God) abides in you, then you will abide in the Son and in the Father" (1Jn 2:23-24), because "whoever confesses that Jesus is the Son of God, God abides in Him, and he in God" (1Jn 4:15).

St. John is talking about a faith in Christ "which is enlivened by love" and is shown in obedience to God's commandments. The mutual abiding of the faithful in God and of God in them is brought about as much by their faith as by their love and their obedience to the divine commandments. "God is love and he who abides in love abides in God, and God abides in him" (1Jn 4:16). "Whoever keeps his [Jesus Christ's] word, in him the love of God is truly perfected. By this we may be sure that we are in him; he who says he abides in him ought to walk in the same way in which he walked" (1Jn 1:5-6). So, faith, love and keeping the commandments are the main "spiritual means" of reaching out to Jesus Christ, of becoming one with him, and through him, of enjoying and sharing in the divine presence he possesses in himself.

Baptism is introduced in the New Testament as a sacred rite, "a sacrament" to which the man of faith is brought by the thrust of his conversion to and faith in

Jesus Christ. Those who repented and confessed that he is the saving Lord were "baptized in the name of Jesus Christ for the forgiveness of sin, so as to receive the gift of the Holy Spirit" (Ac 2:38). Just as faith is the spiritual foundation of the Christian's abiding in Jesus Christ and in God, and of Christ's and God's abiding in him, so baptism actualizes the mutual presence between man and God through Christ in the Holy Spirit.

Jesus himself has joined faith and baptism together as two essential means and necessary conditions for salvation. After his resurrection, he said to his disciples: "Go, and make disciples of all nations; baptize them in the name of the Father, of the Son, and of the Holy Spirit, and teach them to observe all the commands that I have given you" (Mt 28:19-20). The parallel text of St. Mark leaves no doubt about the absolute necessity of faith and baptism for salvation. "He who believes and is baptized will be saved; but he who does not believe will be condemned" (Mk 16:16).

According to St. John, baptism is a mysterious "new birth through water and the Spirit" required for entrance into God's kingdom (Jn 3:5). Baptism takes the man of faith from the darkness of his sinfulness and transports him into the light of Christ (Ep 5:8; 1 P 2:9-10). The union of the faithful with Christ through baptism is no less marked than the union with him brought about by faith. St. Paul wrote a well-known passage about the sacramental grafting of the baptized into Christ. In St. Paul's doctrine, the union between the baptized and Jesus Christ is so intimate that through baptism the former shares mysteriously in the death and resurrection of the latter. "When we were baptized in Christ Jesus we were baptized into his death. In other words, when we were baptized we went into the tomb with him and joined him in death, so that as Christ was raised from the dead by the Father's glory, we too might live a new life" (Rm 6:3-4). All baptized "have clothed themselves in Christ" (Gal 3:27), and can apply to themselves the words that St. Paul used of himself: "I have been crucified with Christ, and I live now not with my own life but with the life of Christ who lives in me. The life I now live in this body, I live in faith: faith in the Son of God who loved me, and who sacrificed himself for my sake" (Gal 2:20). So then, every baptized person has been "joined to the Lord, making one Spirit with him" (1 Cor 6:17); and every baptized Christian is a person for whom "to live is Jesus Christ" (Ph 1:21).

The union of the baptized with Christ is so close that it reaches a kind of mysterious identification with Him. This also makes it possible for anyone grafted into Christ by baptism to actually share the same divine life and divine presence lived and enjoyed by the Lord. Remember the beautiful allegory of St. John: "Make your home in me as I make mine in you. As a branch cannot bear fruit all by itself, but must remain part of the vine, neither can you unless you remain in me. I am the vine, you are the branches. . ." (Jn 15:4-5, ff).

Now let us consider the *most important aspects* of the sharing of God's presence granted to Christians and realized in the Person of Christ. It will be helpful to recall the distinction made between the "tabernacling" and "representative" presence of God.

The "*tabernacling*" presence is perfectly achieved in Christ, and it may be shared by the Christian who is spiritually engrafted to the very Person and Body of Christ. What is first accomplished by baptism attains its most perfect earthly achievement in the Eucharist— through which and in which the Risen Lord keeps his bodily presence in this world. Accordingly, the effects of *baptism* with respect to the union between the baptized and Christ is described as a "complantation" (*symfutoi*)

(Rm 6:5). The *result* of the union between the Christian and Christ in the *Eucharist* is called a "communion" (*koinonia*) (1Cor 10:16). The "tabernacling" presence of God in the Christian finds its deepest and most wondrous achievement on earth in the "Indwelling Presence" of the Holy Trinity, particularly the Holy Spirit. The divine Persons abide in the human person, changing that person into a mystical "temple of God."

God's *"representative"* presence is also brought to its summit in Christ, and the Christian shares in this presence from the very first moment of his baptism, as he participates in the kingly, priestly, and prophetic roles and mission of the Lord. Each Christian truly bears in himself some share in the divine power and presence that God used to reveal through the kings, prophets and priests of the Old Testament, and which he both renewed and perfected in Christ Jesus. Every Christian bears this reflection in a different way and degree, according to his personal charism and office in the Church. We cannot doubt this sharing by Christians in the "representative" presence of God achieved in Christ through his prophetic and royal priesthood (1P 2:4-10).

The Christian also shares in God's presence in Christ through imitation of Jesus' role as the "Suffering Servant," beside whom God stands with special benevolence and concern. Every Christian *ought* to be a follower of Christ, carrying his cross behind the Lord, and so becoming a living image of the Crucified Savior. God the Father looks upon such Christians with the same benevolence that he showed toward Jesus dying on the Cross. This loving, caring attention is a special form of the divine presence realized in someone who is needy, humble and surrenders to God — such as were the "poor of Yahweh" in the Old Testament. The image of Christ that such needy, hungry, poor people carry imprinted upon themselves is so much like their model that he identifies himself with "each one of the least of these brothers" of his. At the Last Judgment, we shall all be judged on what we did for these hungry, thirsty, naked people as if we had done it to Jesus himself (Mt 25:31-46).

Indwelling Presence

The most excellent, consoling and ennobling form of God's presence granted to the Christian on this earth is the *indwelling presence* of the Most Holy Trinity. This form of presence is also granted through Jesus Christ, and seems to be related both to the "tabernacling" presence of the Old Testament and to its perfection in the hypostatic union at the outset of the New Testament. The indwelling presence develops in the Christian an intimate, interior fullness of the local "tabernacling" presence of the Old Testament, and appears as some kind of participation by the Christian in the hypostatic union realized in Christ Jesus between his human nature and the divine Person of the only Son of God.

The *hypostatic union* is that form of God's presence which makes the man Jesus Christ the "only Son of God." Likewise, the indwelling presence makes the Christian an "adopted son of God." All adopted children of God are such in and through their union with the Only-Begotten Son. Therefore, the unique mediation between God and man exercised by Jesus plays a decisive role in bringing to fulfillment the "tabernacling" presence of the Old Testament, as well as its change into the indwelling presence of the New Testament.

We can see that the "tabernacling" presence, localized in a temple of stone throughout the Old Testament, is now assumed into the hypostatic union which characterizes the human-divine being of Jesus Christ. In Jesus this presence can be shared by all who are one with him through faith and baptism. This deeply "personal" presence of God is called in the New Testament the "indwelling Presence." So intimate and personal a form of God's presence constitutes the most grounded and deep foundation of the mystical union with God which a Christian can reach in contemplative prayer. Indeed, such prayer is precisely a very simple and penetrating human insight into God who has made his home in the depths of the loving Christian's heart.

The Holy Spirit in the Indwelling Presence

All our previous considerations were inspired by the New Testament teaching that faith disposes the Christian to receive from the *Father* the indwelling presence of *Jesus Christ*, insofar as this same Christian is "planted and built up in love,"—a love which is infused by the *Holy Spirit* (Ep 3:14-19). The entire Trinity, therefore, dwells within the believing and loving Christian, although at times only one or two of the Persons is said to abide.

The *indwelling presence* is attributed in a particular way to the *Holy Spirit*. He has a very special connection with divine love, and *that* is the most perfect and necessary predisposition required of the human person in order to receive God's abiding presence within. John the Baptist foretold that Jesus Christ would baptize his disciples "with the Holy Spirit and fire" (Mt 3:11; Mk 1:8; Lk 3:16; Jn 1:33-34). The *Acts of the Apostles* testify to an abundant infusion of the Holy Spirit into the baptized (Ac 8:17; 2:38). St. Paul writes that God "saved us by means of the cleansing water of rebirth and by renewing us with the Holy Spirit which he has so generously poured over us through Jesus Christ our Savior" (Tt 3:5-6ff; 1Cor 6:11; Ep 5:25-26). Jesus, who was conceived by the power of the Holy Spirit and "to whom God gives the Spirit without reserve" (Jn 3:34), promised those who believed in him that the Spirit would flow copiously from them "like fountains of living water" (Jn 7:38). The same promise is expressed during Jesus' address to his disciples at the Last Supper (Jn 14:17; 15:26; 16:17). The Holy Spirit is given to the Apostles so that they may with wisdom and power lead and govern the Church (Ac 5:9; 15-28). But the same Spirit is poured out upon *all* the faithful on the day of Pentecost (Ac 2:1-4). Hence, St. Paul could write that "God himself has anointed us, marking us with his seal and giving us the pledge, the Spirit, that we carry in our hearts" (2Cor 1:21-22; Ep 1:13-14; 4:30). In a word, the "Spirit of God has made his home in us" (Rm 8:9). Consequently, St. Paul teaches that the very body of a Christian is the temple of the Holy Spirit. "Your body, you know, is the temple of the Holy Spirit who is in you since you received him from God. You are not your own property; you have been bought and paid for. That is why you should use your body for the glory of God" (1Cor 6:19-20).

The Holy Spirit and the Individual Christian

Each Christian is a *"personal"* temple wherein there can and ought to be celebrated that interior spiritual worship foretold by the prophets for the messianic era. With the Coming of Christ, as Jesus himself assured the Samaritan woman at the well, "the hour is already here when true worshippers will worship the Father in spirit and in truth. . . God is Spirit, and those who worship must worship in spirit and truth" (Jn 4:23-24).

Baptism brings about a mysterious presence of the Holy Spirit which is like an anointing, a seal, and a pledge. Or better still, in baptism, a divine Person makes his abode, takes possession and consecrates the baptized person into a mystical temple of God. But the Holy Spirit is the gift of the Father, and the "Spirit of Christ." Therefore, the Father and Son also come to abide in this spiritual temple consecrated by the Holy Spirit within the Christian.

The infusion of divine love is particularly attributed to the Spirit (Rm 5:5; Gal 5:22; 2 Cor 6:6). The same divine love which enlivens and binds the divine Persons to one another in the circumincession of the Holy Trinity overflows into the Christian, and brings to him the indwelling of these divine Guests. "We can know that we are living in him and he is living in us because he lets us share his Spirit. . . God is love and he who lives in love lives in God, and God lives in him" (1Jn 4:13, 16). "If anyone loves me" says Jesus, "he will keep my word, and my Father will love him, and we shall come to him and make our home with him. . . and the Advocate, the Holy Spirit, whom the Father will send in My name will teach you everything" (Jn 14:23, 26). We see in this passage that the love infused by the Spirit into the Christian to prepare in him a home or a temple for the Holy Trinity is not separated from "knowledge." It is by the Spirit of Truth who issues from the Father (Jn 15:26; cf. 1Jn 5:6 "Since the Spirit is the Truth") that the Christian acquires the true knowledge of Jesus Christ and his redemptive mystery (1Cor 2:10-16; Ep 3:5).

By virtue of this marvelous indwelling of the Holy Trinity, each Christian already possesses, in the darkness of faith, that eternal presence of God which will be realized perfectly in heaven. In St. John's Gospel, Jesus uses the word "house" (*mone*) to describe the indwelling

presence, and the same word is used by him for the
heavenly abode with the Father to which Jesus will take
his disciples after His death. The Christian response to
God making his "home" within us is one of love,
knowledge and prayer. Actually, the mystery of this
indwelling is the deepest center and origin of all personal
loving awareness of God's presence brought into action
by Christian prayer. It is the prayer of those who, through
the Spirit, have become the adopted children of God.
They have learned from the Spirit to address themselves
in prayer to God with the word "Abba," as Jesus Christ
the only Son of God used to pray. It is worth noting that
"Abba" is like "daddy" in English, a word of familiarity
and endearment originating in the prattling of children.

> Everyone moved by the Spirit is a son of God. The
> Spirit you received is not the Spirit of slaves bringing
> fear into your lives again; it is the Spirit of sons, and it
> makes us cry out "Abba!", "Father!" The Spirit
> Himself and our spirit bear united witness that we are
> children of God. . . The Spirit too comes to help us in
> our weakness. For when we cannot choose words in
> order to pray properly, the Spirit Himself expresses
> our plea in a way that could never be put into words,
> and God Who knows everything in our hearts knows
> perfectly well what we mean, and the pleas of the
> saints expressed by the Spirit are according to the
> mind of God (Rm 8:14-17,26-27; Gal 4:5-6).

The Community of the Faithful

The indwelling presence of God, although a clearly
individual grace, is not at all individualistic. On the

contrary, when God's presence is established within the Christian as his indwelling or abiding presence it makes the recipient a living member of the Church, the community of the faithful. What occurs in each Christian holds true also for *the whole community made up of all Christians together.* The Holy Trinity abides also within the whole Church founded by Christ, beloved of the Father and enlivened by the Holy Spirit.

Individual baptism lies at the very origin and foundation of the Church, for it establishes the basic unity of the Christian with Jesus. The baptized person is "indwelt" by the Holy Spirit. "In the one Spirit we were all baptized. . .and one Spirit was given to us all to drink" (1Cor 12:13). "You are, all of you, sons of God through faith in Christ Jesus. All baptized in Christ, you have all clothed yourselves in Christ, and there are no more distinctions between Jew and Greek, slave and free, male and female, but all of you are one in Christ Jesus" (Gal 3:26-28). "There is one Body, one Spirit. . .There is one Lord, one faith, one baptism, and one God who is the Father of all, over all, through all and within all!" (Ep 4:4-6). In these passages we find one of the most typical considerations of St. Paul: the church is "the Body of Christ."

The people of Israel had described their intimacy with God, i.e., the mutual loving-presence that God and the people had established with one another, under the image of marriage. In the same way, Jesus Christ loves and unites the Church to himself as the bridegroom actualizes "in one flesh" the union with his bride (Ep 5:22-27). Therefore Christ, as husband with respect to his wife, is said to be "the head of the Church" (Ep 5:23), while "the Church is his body" (Col 1:18, 24; Ep 5:29). Christ and the Church are actually identified as if they were the same person: "Just as a human body, though it is made up of many parts, is a single unit, because all these parts, though many, make one body, so it is with Christ. In one Spirit we were all baptized. . ." (1Cor 12:12-13). The context of the last passage shows that St. Paul is directly speaking about the members of the Church. However, he does not conclude that the Church is made up by its members, but that Christ himself is formed by them. An identification such as this manifests how deep and total in Pauline teaching is the "oneness" of Christ with the Christians who comprise his Church. Indeed, all Christians "together are Christ's body" (1Cor 12:27), or better yet, their bodies "are members making up the body of Christ" (1Cor 6:15), as "its living parts" (Ep 5:29).

Christ is the "head that adds strength and holds the whole body together, with all its joints and sinews—and this is the only way it can reach its full growth in God" (Col 2:19). Eventually, "there is no room for distinction between Greek and Jew, between uncircumcised and circumcised, or between barbarian and Scythian, slave and free man. There is only one Christ: he is everything and he is in everything" (Col 3:11). And "just as each of our bodies has several parts and each part a separate function, so all of us in union with Christ, form one body, and as part of it we belong to each other" (Rm 1:4-5; Col 3:15; Ep 4:25).

Such teaching provides a clear framework of truth: in an encounter through faith and love, the Christian can and must acknowledge the mysterious, real presence of Christ and God in each one of his brothers. This presence is particularly to be noted in those who have taken over the mission of the apostles (Lk 10:15 "I am with you [the apostles] always; yes, to the end of time"; Mt 28: 20, in those who are poor and needy, Mt 25:40, in children, Mk 9:27; Mt 18:5; Lk 9:48). There is a maxim not recorded in the canonical Gospels yet attributed to Christ by some of

the early Christian writers, and it seems to sum up several
sayings of the Lord: "Have you seen a brother? You have
seen God!" (St. Clement of Alexandria, Stromata I, 19
and II, 15, 17; Tertullian, *De Oratione*, 26).

Christian Community and Prayer

If prayer is yearning after and loving awareness of
God's presence wherever it may be found, then a truth
such as the one quoted above can constantly enkindle and
nourish Christian prayer. Whenever the faithful meet,
work, converse with one another, Christ is present. On the
other hand, the same presence of Jesus and of God in the
Christian community and in the various groups of people
living in it ought to inspire and sustain worship and
prayer. This is confirmed by the simile of the "Temple of
God" which, as a house of prayer, is built by the faithful as
with living stones. In fact, such a simile is applied to the
Church with symbolism parallel to that of the "Body of
Christ."

> Through Christ we have access in one Spirit to the
> Father. So you are no longer aliens or foreigners, but
> you are citizens with the saints, and part of God's
> household. You are part of a building that has the
> apostles and prophets for its foundations, and Christ
> Jesus himself for its main cornerstone. As every
> structure is aligned on him, all grow into one holy
> temple in the Lord; and you too, in him, are being
> built into a house where God lives in the Spirit (Ep
> 2:19-22).

Notice the explicit mention of the Holy Trinity which

gives unity and life to the Church, at the beginning and end of this passage.

The similes of "God's temple" and of "God's household" are intimately intertwined with one another. They recall the abiding presence of Yahweh among his people, in the "household of David" and within the temple of Jerusalem. Therefore, the entire community of the faithful is said to be changed into the true Israel of God (Rm 2:28-29; Gal 6:16; Ph 3:3) "a chosen race, a royal priesthood, a consecrated nation, a people set apart" (1 Pt 2:9; Is 43:20-21). Where once the ancient and frequently repeated promise of God to abide "as a Father in the midst of his people" sustained hope (Lv 26:12; Ezk 37:27; Is 52:11; Ho 1:10; 2 S 7:14) there is now final fulfillment: (Gal 3:29: "We are the temple of the living God. We have God's word for it: I will make my house among them and live with them; I will be their God and they will be my people. . ." (2Cor 2:16 = Lv 26:11-12) and I will welcome you and be your Father, and you shall be my sons and daughters, says the Almighty Lord" (2Cor 2:18 = Is 43:6).

The sacred character of the mystical temple of God, i.e., the Church indwelt by God, and the duty of the same Church to offer sacrifices and prayers to God present within it, are logical consequences of this wonderful mystery. "Do you not realize that you are God's temple and that the Spirit of God dwells among you? If anyone should destroy the temple of God, God will destroy him, because the temple of God is sacred, and you are that temple" (1Cor 3:16-17).

Eucharist: Center of Worship and Source of Church's Unity

"Set yourselves close to him (i.e., Jesus Christ) so that

you too, the holy priesthood that offers the spiritual sacrifices which Jesus Christ has made acceptable to God, may be living stones making a spiritual house" (1 Pt 2:4-5). In the context of Christian worship, the Eucharist— permanent "real" presence of Jesus Christ in the midst of the Church — constitutes at one and the same time the center of Christian worship and prayer, and the food and drink nourishing the unity of the Church in a single body through the communion of each and every member in Christ. "The blessing-cup that we bless is a communion with the blood of Christ, and the bread that we break is a communion with the body of Christ. The fact that there is only one loaf means that, though there are many of us, we form a single body because we all have a share in this one loaf" (1 Cor 10:16-17).

Through his Eucharistic food and drink, Jesus Christ feeds the entire Church with his very person. his real presence is sown, so to speak, in the body and spirit of all Christians like a seed of divine, eternal life which will one day bring the entire Church to final resurrection. "Anyone who eats my flesh and drinks my blood has eternal life, and I shall raise him up on the last day. . . he who eats my flesh and drinks my blood lives in Me and I live in him. As I who am sent by the living Father, myself draw life from the Father, so whoever eats me will draw life from me. This is the bread come down from heaven. . . Anyone who eats this bread will live forever (Jn 6:54-58). Whenever Christians eat and drink the Body and Blood of Jesus Christ, they do so as a memorial of his death "Until the Lord will come" to share with them his own glory (1 Cor 11:24-26). The Eucharistic presence is completely projected towards the second Coming of Jesus Christ to earth, at the end of time, when he will reveal himself unveiled and glorious to all His faithful who have been raised by virtue of his Resurrection.

Christians truly are grafted onto the very person of Christ. They are fed by his Body and Blood. They are indwelt by the Holy Trinity. They are consecrated into a holy people and temple of God where the divine presence abides. Yet, notwithstanding all these lofty graces, and filled with confidence because of the pledge of the Spirit given to them, they still "remember that to live in the body means to be exiled from the Lord, going as they do by faith and not by sight. Therefore they want to be exiled from the body and make their home with the Lord" (2Cor 5:5-8). Only then, in fact, will they enjoy the presence of God not "as a dim reflection in a mirror but face to face," and they will know him "as fully as they are known" (1Cor 13:12).

When human time and earthly history will be no more, the entire Church will be changed into the "holy city, and the new Jerusalem, coming down from God out of heaven, as beautiful as a bride all dressed for her husband—where God lives among men. He will make his home among them; they shall be His people and He will be their God; his name is God—with—them. He will wipe away all tears from their eyes; there will be no more mourning and sadnrss. The world of the past has gone" (Rv 21:2-4). But meanwhile, a fervent prayer is constantly addressed by the Church to the Lord through his abiding Spirit: "The Spirit and the Bride say, 'Come.' Let everyone who listens answer, 'Come'. . . Come, Lord Jesus!" (Rv 22:17, 20).

The presence of God revealed to man throughout the many centuries of salvation history traversed by the *Bible* is a *totally gratuitous and freely offered self-giving of God to man.* As far as God's presence is concerned, man can do nothing save open his mind and heart to it, letting the divine presence enter his own life. In the poetical imagery of the *Book of Revelation*, "Look," says Christ, "I am standing at the door knocking. If one of you hears me calling and opens the door, I will come in to share his meal, side by side with him" (Rv 3:20). In the Christian religion, therefore, man's spiritual efforts, exercises and training are never, of themselves, able to create (as out of nothing) or capture with a compelling power any experience of God's presence. Man can only strive to open himself and be responsive to this presence which, as the effect of great divine benevolence, is already knocking at the door of his heart and life. In short, God is always the first to become involved in his presence to man, and man's response is always second. So, the human experience of God's presence is more *receptive* than creative, since the "objectivity" of God's presence is primary, and the subjective human detection of it follows and is secondary.

The revelation and realization of God's presence to man is described in the *Bible* as a *progressive development*. The main thrusts constantly followed in this development are:

— from multiplicity to unity;
— from communal to personal experience;
— from outwardness to inwardness.

The most perfect achivements of all these processes in revealing God's presence are found in Jesus Christ. In the mysterious divine and human Person of Christ, we see that:

—All material symbols of God's presence, so widely spread throughout the Old Testament, reach their perfect unity.
—In him, God's presence becomes highly personal, not only in a "psychological" but in a deep

"metaphysical" sense. Indeed, the tradition of the Church speaks of a "hypostatic (personal) union" between man and God in Jesus Christ.
—In him the human experience of God's presence is innermost; Christ simply identifies himself with God: "The Father and I are one."

The constant, manifold development of God's presence throughout the *Bible* follows a course of *addition and improvement*: earlier forms of the divine presence move toward more perfect ones. In making himself more and more present to man, God never contradicts himself. He never retracts from His previous promises. Therefore, the innermost personal, unique presence of God achieved in Christ Jesus is not a rejection of the external communal presence God realized and revealed during the Old Testament era. In Christ the divine presence reaches its most perfect accomplishment. What in the Old Testament had been the "material," "local" tabernacling presence of God now attains its peak "corporal-personal" realization in the very *being* of Jesus Christ. This is true of Jesus both in his risen condition and under the Eucharistic species. God's presence among his people is equally fulfilled in the Christian community, "the mystical body of Christ," in a manner that is still communal but much more interior than before the coming of Christ.

The same thing happens in the individual Christian, who certainly enjoys the indwelling presence of the Holy Trinity in a very intimate, personal manner. However, God's presence does not limit itself to man's spirit alone; it overflows into man's body, making it also a "temple of the Holy Spirit." Eventually, through the same Holy Spirit who acts as the Soul of the Church, each Christian is transformed into a living cell of the Mystical Body of Christ.

During this final age of redemptive history, various aspects of God's presence are realized through Christ in the Christian and in the Church: they are simultaneously corporal, outward (as in the Body of Christ in the Eucharist, in the body of the Christian, in the Church) and spiritual, intimate (as in the "hypostatic union," in the spirit of man where the Holy Trinity dwells as in its home, in the ecclesial communion effected by the Spirit of Love). This divine presence is individual-personal, and communal-ecclesial, as in the many persons representing Christ (apostles, the poor, children). It is extremely simple or actually one, because it is always the same presence of God, shared in and through Christ. These apparently opposite aspects and characteristics of God's presence not only do not exclude, but they positively *include* one another. This last era of salvation history, inaugurated by Jesus Christ, is the most perfect era before the Parousia. It is an era of accomplishment and of synthesis, as much as one of revelation and actualization of the divine presence.

Another qualification of God's presence shows up clearly since the time of the prophets and is re-inforced by Christ and the apostles' preaching in the New Testament. This is what we call its "eschatological orientation." God's presence fulfilled in and through Jesus Christ is already perfect. But it is not yet so perfected in fullness and extension in the rest of creation as it is destined to be at the end of time when God will be ALL in all things. The full incorporation of each Christian and of the whole Church into the Risen and Glorified Lord is not yet actualized. We are still mortal beings, and we can still separate ourselves from God and from Christ before our death.

Also, though the intimate indwelling of the Holy Trinity in our persons is real and most wonderful, we still do not enjoy the unveiled vision and possession of the divine Persons, since we live enfolded in the darkness of faith.

The task of Christian prayer is precisely to increase, day by day, in the awareness of God's presence in Christ during this eschatological era of ours. It will help us to advance more rapidly, to effectively cover the distance which separates us from that future meeting with the full unveiled presence of God. Such is the meeting we are invited to enjoy eternally in heaven.

CHAPTER 3

THEOLOGY OF GOD'S PRESENCE AND CHRISTIAN PRAYER

In previous chapters we gathered from the *Bible* the "raw material" for building a systematic theology of God's presence in and through Christ. Some other contributions to elaborate that theology can be taken from human cultural experience and thought.

To work out a brief but systematic Christian theology of the divine presence, we shall follow the outlines of our Creed, in whose articles are summarized all the fundamental Christian truths taught in the *Bible*. Christian prayer *is* the awareness of the full mystery of God, expressed and described briefly in the Creed. The most important moments in divine revelation which make known and establish God's presence among his people are:

Creation — The fact of creation establishes within all creatures a presence of God as creator, and this presence is particularly attributed to the *Father*.
Salvation — This mystery of God's mercy is the foundation of a presence of God among men as Savior: manifested and personified by the only *Son of*

God made man, Jesus Christ.

Sanctification — The presence of God as Sanctifier, realized by the accomplishment of Salvation within each individual Christian is especially attributed to the *Holy Spirit*.

Each of these principal mysteries of faith is both an important "act" in the whole drama of salvation history and an essential "truth" of the Christian Creed. We shall consider in detail each mystery and the particular form of God's presence involved in it.

Creation

The creation of the whole universe by God the Father is emphasized from the very first solemn statement in the Christian Creed:

> We believe in one God, the Father, the Almighty, maker of heaven and earth, of all that is seen and unseen.

Traditional Christian theology strove to better understand this mystery by means of the metaphysical concept of causality. God, the Creator, is the *source* (or first "efficient cause"), the *archetype*, (or primary "exemplary cause"), the goal, (or ultimate "final cause") of all creatures. The innumerable created beings of the universe are permeated through and through by such divine creative causality. All creatures depend on the divine creative action as they first come into existence, during the time they exist as real beings, and in all the developments they undergo. Before coming into being, all creatures were simply nothing. An infinite distance had to be covered to take them from nothingness into being, and only Almighty God has the infinite power required to cover that "distance." All creatures necessarily need God's loving and caring presence to begin their existence, and to be what they are.

Even after passing the threshold of being, creatures still need God's creative influence and support. Their radical kinship with nothingness continually drives them back towards it. There is something within them which acts like a force of gravity: it persistently pulls them "downwards" and constantly exposes them to the danger of falling back into the abyss of nothingness. God must always be there to "pull them out"—even against their natural thrust towards nothingness. Such activity of Almighty God keeps all creatures in the realm of being by the persistence of that same loving care which he manifested when he first created them. It is called *"conservation."* Together with the "call from nothingness," creatures also show a drive towards the fullness of their being, or a "call towards perfection." Creatures need God for their very being and its continuation; they need him for developing their potentialities and for making any kind of progress. They desperately need God's *increasing influence* in order to obtain the extra energies required to move onwards and eventually reach the goal of their being. It is the deep yearning to become as similar as possible to, or better yet, less dissimilar from God, which calls the creature to move towards its final end. This end is God himself—even though his absolute transcendence impedes every creature from attaining him by its own natural force.

The very being, persistence and progress of all creatures would be metaphysically impossible if the all-pervading and powerful action, influence and support of God were not always present to sustain them. Yet, in no sense is God himself "captured" or fused with his creatures. This is the deep ontological significance of the Christian dogma of Creation.

Different Modes of God's Presence To Creation

The above explanation of revealed truth makes clear how deep, real and enduring is God's creative, conservative and progressive presence. God is where he acts in all creatures and in the whole universe. Nothing is deeper, more real, or more enduring in any creature than the core of its very being where only God acts and is inwardly present. Consequently, the being and constant evolution of the universe and of each creature in it should give evidence to every Christian of the God who is present and abides in the very depths of all creatures who live out their faith in a conscious and illumined way. Especially during prayer, such faith should make the Christian vibrantly and gratefully aware of God's creative presence within himself and in all creatures of this world.

God the Creator may be compared to a workman or an artist. What God creates is full of wisdom and beauty, and these qualities extend to creatures—like a glimpse of the original Beauty and Wisdom of God himself. One should "see," then, the presence of a beautiful and wise Creator in his creatures. However, the simile of an artist is defective, for usually a work of art outlives its maker. The human artist imprints only a form of beauty upon something whose being does not depend on him. So the work of art continues in being even after the artist's death. But as we mentioned above, creatures cannot persist in being without the constant, creative, conservative and progressive action of God who stands always at the very core of their being and sustains them.

A more adequate similitude to clarify the idea of God's creative presence is taken from those phenomena which, as long as they are real, depend constantly and totally on the originating *cause* of their being. Such, for example, are daylight caused by the rising sun, or a river's stream flowing from the merger of many springs, or speech proceeding from the human mouth, or the experience of being loved caused by a loving person. These phenomena may be used as suitable examples to emphasize the constant influence and presence of God's creative power at work in all creatures. But they still remain thoroughly inadequate to demonstrate the absolute separation which marks God off from all his created beings.

Of course, God the Creator is always present as the "ground of being" at the "deepest depth" of his creatures. But he remains substantially separated from them because, against any form of pantheism, creatures are not God, and God cannot be identified with any of them. So, God's creative presence in the world is a great mystery of innermost immanence coupled with utmost transcendence. God is "more intimate than I am to myself, and higher than the highest peak of my being" as St. Augustine aptly expresses.

Origin of Diverse Modes of Divine Presence

We have considered the many forms of divine presence which exist among the countless creatures of our universe. Now we may ask whence these differentiations originate? And on what are they founded? Certainly, the first reason for this manifold difference is *God's free choice* in willing many and diverse creatures.

The main ontological foundation of the diverse ways in which the divine creative presence appears resides in the *very being of each creature:* in its own nature and degree of perfection or similarity to God. We can imagine that creatures are like tiny fragments of that huge mirror which stands before God as the universe. Each creature catches a little ray or trace of the infinite shining glory of God. More perfect creatures are better reflections of God and show that the divine creative presence is more involved in their being. Human beings are created as "images" of God, while all other creatures are only his "footprints." Even though an image may be darkened or blurred, it is still better than a footprint in making known the person who left behind signs of his passing. An image always brings us closer to the presence of the person represented.

The reality of this multi-faceted creative presence of God ought to be a constant stimulus to prayer. Any form of God's presence calls for the loving awareness which is typical of prayer. The faith-insight of the Christian penetrates deeply into creatures, and detects in them a presence of God, the Creator—thus inspiring prayer. The explanation of this mystery which we have elaborated can nourish Christian prayer by means of reasoning and imagination. In this way, they help a prayerful Christian to keep as vibrant as possible his insightful awareness of God's creative presence—everywhere and in everything. For the fact of the matter is that among all creatures, God's creative presence is especially found in man himself. "From the very circumstances of his origin, man is already invited to converse with God. For man would not exist were he not created by God's love and constantly preserved by it. And he cannot live fully according to truth unless he freely acknowledges that love and devotes himself to his Creator" (*Gaudium et* Spes # 19).

God's creative presence is spread over the entire universe, which ought to be brought back to its Creator through *human praise and obedience.* "Through his bodily composition man gathers to himself the elements of the material world. Thus they reach their crown through him; and through him raise their voice in free praise of the Creator" (GS # 14). "For man, created to God's image, received a mandate to subject to himself the earth and all that it contains, and to govern the world with justice and holiness; a mandate to relate himself and the totality of things to him who was to be acknowledged as the Lord and Creator of all. Thus, by subjection of all things to man, the name of God would be wonderful in all the earth" (GS # 34). Undoubtedly, an atheist insofar as he is blind to God, cannot "see" God's creative presence in the universe. A distracted or disinterested Christian can fail to "see" it, as if he, too, were a "practical" atheist. Atheism is one of the most poisonous fruits of present-day civilization, as we shall explain in the next chapter.

Salvation in Christ

Christians also believe in Christ's salvation. The Creed describes briefly the whole mystery of salvation:

We believe in one Lord, Jesus Christ, the only Son of God... begotten, not made, and one in being with the Father... through him all things were made... For us men and our salvation he came down from heaven... and became man. For our sake he was crucified, suffered, died and was buried. On the third day he rose again. . . He ascended into heaven and is seated at the right hand of the Father. . . He will come in glory to judge the living and the dead, and his kingdom will have no end.

The saving presence of Jesus Christ as Son of God, Incarnate Savior and eschatological Lord (indicated in these articles of faith) marvelously surpasses God's creative presence by developing, concretizing and extending the revelation and realization of it throughout the whole of human history from its beginnings until the end of time.

To elaborate theologically this saving presence of Christ within human history, it will be useful to make a fundamental distinction: Jesus Christ is both (a) a *mystery of faith*, and (b) a *sacrament* of Salvation. As a *mystery*, Jesus Christ is *the* "crucial event" within human history in which God personally encounters mankind. Man needs to acknowledge and welcome God in and through Christ by the personal assent of faith in his mystery. It must be a faith which grows into hope and charity. As a *sacrament*, Jesus Christ is the primordial "sacred sign" and instrument of God's Salvation. He is a kind of a "super-sacrament" bringing divine salvation to all men through their "bodily" contact with him, and their vital grafting onto him as Savior. The existential response of faith and the ontological reception of the sacraments together make up the full actualization of Christ's saving presence in the Church.

The saving presence of Jesus Christ as a mystery of faith has a multi-faceted richness. Jesus is certainly in the *whole universe*: since he is one with the Father, he is always involved with him in the work of creation. Therefore Christian theology attributes to Jesus Christ a specific creative role and presence in the universe. The Old Testament emphasizes that the universe was created by God's "word" and "wisdom." And in the New Testament, Jesus is identified with God's "Word" and "Truth," so that "through Jesus Christ all things were made." Jesus shares with God the Father in his creative presence to each creature and to the whole of creation. This creative presence provides a groundwork for salvation; i.e., for the "re-creation" of mankind and of the entire universe.

The human nature which the only Son of God assumed hypostatically in Jesus Christ makes him present in a special way to mankind. Since the Son of God became man in Jesus, every human being is, in and through him, a brother of the Son of God. Thus, Jesus can identify himself with the "least of his brothers." The Incarnation also adds a new dimension to his presence in the material universe, which is the natural environment of mankind. Man is a microcosm who wonderfully sums up in his body all the elements of the material world. When the Son of God became man, in some way he assumed into himself the whole material universe. Put in another but equivalent way: Jesus Christ is mysteriously—through the material elements of His human body—in all material beings, which are to some extent "consecrated" by his Incarnation.

The saving presence of the only Son of God made man in Christ, a real man among other men, makes him the apex of all *human history*. This is particularly true because of his actual position as Risen Lord: he is the ultimate fulfillment of all human history. Christ already possesses that final glory to which mankind is tending as towards its final goal. He is the divine-human source of Salvation, drawing all human history to its completion. Christ also mysteriously leads, governs, and saves man throughout history, exerting his roles of King, Prophet and Priest. From his fullness, each one of us constantly receives grace upon grace, as from the caring presence of an all-powerful and self-giving Savior.

All these modes of Christ's saving presence in the world, in mankind, in human history, brought about by his Incarnation, Death and Resurrection, are objectively (though mysteriously) real. But they are not self-evident, nor self-operating. Unbelievers cannot "see," "meet," and be saved by them. Only the Christian who recognizes them through faith, hope and charity experiences the manifold saving influence of Jesus as Savior. The presence of Christ requires human acceptance in order to become God's saving presence in action and to yield to men the fruits of salvation.

The facets of Jesus' saving presence in the world, in mankind, in human history, may be seen as if arranged in a pyramidal order. The presence of Christ in human history, representing the source and completion of salvation, is like the apex, where the other modes of his saving presence reach their climax. At that apex, the saving presence of Jesus is not only a "mystery of faith" but it is also a "sacrament of Salvation" offered to all mankind.

Jesus, Primordial Sacrament

The saving presence of Jesus as primordial sacrament (i.e., as the first sign and most effective instrument) of salvation, concerns directly and chiefly his *human nature*, his bodily existence as Risen Lord. All God's saving influence on mankind flows "sacramentally" from the fullness of grace concentrated in the Risen Lord. This fullness of grace *is* our shared divine life! But for men who are still living on earth as pilgrims and exiles far from their Father's house, Jesus who "reigns at the right hand of the Father" is not visible and tangible—as an event and sacrament of salvation must be. Therefore, at the moment of his Ascension into heaven, Jesus commissioned the community of his disciples, the Church, to carry out on earth his sacramental saving action and presence until the end of time.

The saving presence of Christ as central event and primordial sacrament of salvation occurs for all men still living on earth in and through the Church. The Church is the Mystical Body of Christ, the visible earthly extension and realization of her invisible Lord's saving presence and power. The Church as a whole is also, in union with Christ, the primordial event and sacrament of salvation. She keeps in her maternal womb the Word of God and the seven sacraments, and with them she shares the divine life or grace which flows from Jesus Christ to all those saved by him.

Church as Sacrament

We shall try to sketch this complex sacramental pattern of the Church in a few broad strokes. The Church is a "sacrament" precisely when taken as a *whole*, as the *community* of all the faithful. "By her relationship with Christ, the Church is a kind of sacrament or sign of intimate union with God, and of the unity of all mankind. She is also an instrument for the achievement of such union and unity." These words found at the beginning of Vatican Council II's *Dogmatic Constitution of the Church*, set the tone for the other documents published by the same Council.

The traditional teaching on the sacraments, conceived

both as revealing signs and effective instruments wherein Christ's saving presence comes into the open and operates, is fully applied to the whole Church. The intimate relationship of the Church with Christ is given as the basic reason for making such an application. This saving presence of Christ among men can be brought about by every Christian community, whatever its size or type of witness may be, in the environment in which it lives. Vatican Council II speaks of local Churches (dioceses, parishes), the first small groups of faithful in mission territories, of Christian families, of religious communities and other groups. All of these Christian communities realize and carry on the saving "sacramental" presence of Christ throughout human history everywhere on earth.

A truth such as this bears important consequences for the prayer life of the contemporary Christian. That loving awareness of God's presence which defines prayer must be sought for and nourished today perhaps more than in the past, in and within Christian communities, in and within the Church. The many forms of prayer (liturgical, communal, charismatic, shared) spreading in our present-day Church and society, respond to contemporary man's leanings and needs.

If Christian prayer today were to take a *merely* individual approach to God's saving presence in Christ, it would be looked upon with suspicion, as if it were "individualistic" in the negative, derogatory sense, and in some way anti-Christian. Such a critical attitude towards private prayer is both false and excessive. Nevertheless, the liturgical renewal and the vast variety of prayer groups and prayer meetings common today appear as important signs of the times. Today the presence of Christ carries on its work of salvation among men *better* in and through a Christian community, which makes his presence more real and acceptable to contemporary man who is himself so socially oriented.

Sacramental Power of Christ Expressed Through Individuals

The Church exerts the sacramental power of her Risen Lord not only as a whole and not only through the various and numerous groups belonging to her. Many persons within the Church share in and exert sacramental saving power by virtue of Christ's presence. The pope, bishops, priests, and deacons, who make up the hierarchy, are all consecrated persons through whose ministry the sacramental saving power and presence of Jesus is manifested in the Church. Christ himself promised to be in and with them until the end of time. The role and mission of Christ as King, Prophet and Priest of the new People of God is carried out by the ecclesial hierarchy insofar as it acts in the name of and with the authority of Christ. The hierarchy provides vicars of Christ who serve as his earthly substitutes to spread Christian salvation among men.

Through baptism, all the faithful also share in the kingly, prophetic, priestly power and saving presence of Jesus Christ. They are enabled to spread Christian salvation in their lives and in the world in the name of and by the authority of their Savior, Jesus. Each and every member of the Church participates to some degree in the sacramental power of presence of the Lord. The difference in this manifold participation regards only the proper range and the specific goals of this shared power and presence.

The *hierarchy*, in different degrees, shares in the

saving, sacramental power and presence of Christ as "*Head*" of the Church. The predominant goal of their ministry is the *communication of that divine life which flows from Jesus Christ the Head* to all men, but particularly to Christians who are already living members of his Mystical Body, the Church.

The *faithful* share in the saving sacramental power and presence of Christ as ordinary "*members*" of the Church. Their role and goal consist in using that power and presence *to dedicate to God, in and through Christ, their human existence and its environment.* While the mission of the hierarchy can be briefly and directly described as the "*sanctification of men*," the role of the faithful consists chiefly in the "*consecration of the world.*" Both hierarchy and faithful, in exercising their own specific mission and role, are living witnesses to Christ's saving power and presence on earth. Christian prayer should also be stimulated by the believing insight which the faithful can attain from Jesus' sacramental power and presence in all the various members of the Church.

Every Christian, whatever be his position in the Church, is "another Christ." This is true of the ecclesiastical hierarchy. To some extent they identify with Jesus, our Savior, particularly when they actually perform their sacred ministry of salvation. This is also true, although in a different mode, of all Christians who try to imitate the life of Christ, the Holy One of God. It should be quite normal for a Christian to sustain his loving awareness of Christ's saving presence by encounter with his fellow Christians in whom he "sees" through faith a reflection of the saving presence of the Lord sought in prayer. "He who has seen a brother has seen the Lord," the first Christians were wont to say.

The New Testament and Christian tradition have constantly pointed out a particular presence of the Lord in all the poor, the needy, and the suffering of humanity. Becoming man for our salvation, the only Son of God wanted to take upon himself all the pain, deprivation and needs of mankind so that in any human being whatsoever—Christian or non-Christian—who is in a difficult or painful situation, there would always be a mysterious similarity to and presence of Jesus, the "Suffering Lord." All of this occurs even when needy, suffering man does not know Jesus Christ; even when he rejects and does not endure the hardships of his life in union with him.

The words of Jesus are profound and clear: "I tell you solemnly, insofar as you did this (i.e., feed the hungry, clothe the naked, visit the sick and prisoners) to one of the least of these brothers of mine, you did it to Me" (Mt 25:40). A Christian should be able to see Jesus in all poor people who need his help and care. Thus he should generously serve all needy persons with a lively and vivid awareness that his Lord wanted to be identified with them, and that he really is present in them. Christians should serve every man in need in the spirit of a believing and loving attitude of prayer.

All these truths about Christ's "sacramental" presence in men wonderfully harmonize with the aspirations of our times. An others-oriented, social, active tendency often noticeable in contemporary Christians inclines them toward a life spent in the Christian community at the service of mankind. Therefore, the forms of prayer most appreciated today are the communal ones, i.e., those helping to build a "community of charity" from a "community of prayer," and particularly that sort of "prayer-in-action" which inspires and sustains the Christian in social work for the welfare of his fellowmen.

"Word" and "Sacrament"

The saving power and presence of Christ exercised in all the sanctifying instruments entrusted to the Church can be compared with His sacramental presence in the human person, yet only in a secondary manner. These instruments can be summed up in the classical categories of "Word" and "Sacrament." They are rightly distinguished as two different categories of sign and instrument in Christian salvation. However, they should never be separated.

The "Word" involves Christ's saving power and presence exerted and revealed in Holy Scripture, tradition and preaching. The "Word" aims at the salvation of men worked out through the revelation of divine Truth personified in Jesus. In the written, spoken and preached Word of God, Jesus is mysteriously present. He is effectively working out the salvation of all who receive him, listen to and obey him. The proclamation of God's Word, constantly carried out by the Church, has, therefore, a quasi-sacramental efficacy throughout the history of salvation.

What the "Word" inaugurates is eventually fulfilled by the "Sacraments," i.e., by the liturgical celebration of Christian salvation within the Church. The source and apex of this sacramental economy is the Eucharist. In the Eucharist, the saving power and presence of Christ is permanent and substantial, not merely transitory and operative as in the "Word" and in the other sacraments. The Eucharist is indeed both the most precious and effective "Sacrament" of Jesus Christ, and the fullest realization of his "mystery" on earth. And so, the two aspects of "mystery" and "sacrament" distinguished above, find again in the Eucharist their perfect identification. In fact, the Eucharist is not only the most perfect sacrament. It is also Jesus Christ offered to God the Father as the most precious *sacrifice* of salvation. It is granted to all Christians as the substantial divine nourishment of their life and unity in the Church—the "Mystical" Body of Christ—sacramentally fed by his "real" Body and Blood.

It is clear that reading, speaking and listening to God's "Word," and celebrating or partaking in the "Sacramental Liturgy" of the Church requires from the Christian that loving awareness of Christ's saving power and presence which is a worthy attitude of prayer. Neither the "Word" nor the "Sacraments" have any absolute self-effective or quasi-magical power. Without the prayerful attitude of the Christian, neither Word nor Sacraments can reveal the saving presence of Christ which they contain in themselves. Even less can they effect man's salvation. We should not forget that Christian prayer always began with and was constantly nourished by an encounter of the praying person with Jesus Christ, believed to be present through his "Word." Practically all methods of Christian prayer begin with a reading taken from Holy Scripture or from a scriptural commentary. To be able to converse with Jesus, the praying Christian must first listen to his Word, as if to learn Christ's "language" before addressing him directly. The Fathers of the Church rightly used to say, "When I read Holy Scripture, I listen to God; when I pray, I speak and respond to him."

Eventually all Christian prayer reaches its perfection in and through the liturgical celebration of the sacraments. This is especially true of the Eucharist which is sacrifice and sacrament at one and the same time, and in which Christian prayer attains its zenith. Whether private or public, Christian prayer is always joined intimately with Christ's saving and sacrificial power in act until the end of time. Mysteriously or openly, in a remote or proximate manner, Christian prayer is essentially the loving awareness of Christ in living encounter with his presence. Thus it is quite natural that such prayer be essentially related to the sacrament-sacrifice of the Eucharist. For in this sacrament, the saving power and presence of the Lord is substantially and permanently "*real*" within salvation history through the ministry of the Church.

Sanctifying Action of the Holy Spirit

Near the end of our Creed we proclaim:

> We believe in the Holy Spirit, the Lord, the giver
> of life. . .

With these words we confess our faith in that sanctification which takes place through the infusion of divine life within us by the Holy Spirit. Since he is "the giver of the holy life of God," the Holy Spirit is called the Sanctifier, par excellence. Such action of the Spirit causes a special form of God's presence in man: his own sanctifying presence. In previous pages we have considered two other forms of divine presence which appear to man as either predominantly "impersonal," such as the creative presence of God the Father, or as "communal," as is the saving presence of Christ. The sanctifying presence of the Holy Spirit is, on the contrary, chiefly personal and individual. One may be involved in God's creative presence not so much as a person, but merely as a creature. One is taken into Christ's saving presence mainly through the sacramental ministry of the Church. But no one can be sanctified by the Holy Spirit without his indwelling presence experienced as an *individual* and in a very personal, intimate way. St. John and St. Paul both teach that the divine Persons, Father, Son and Holy Spirit, through the mediation of the Holy Spirit, giver of divine life and love, come to abide within the individual Christian.

Sanctifying Presence of Holy Spirit

How does theology attempt to explain this marvelous mystery of faith? What are the foundations for this sanctifying, personal presence of God within the Christian? On the part of God, only his paternal, infinitely gratuitous love can explain such a gift. On the part of man, the deepest disposition enabling him to receive and preserve God's indwelling and sanctifying presence *is* the divine life shared with him by the infusion of the Holy Spirit. Sharing in the very life of God, the Christian is introduced into the mysterious circulation of life, knowledge and love eternally in act among the Three divine Persons.

A Christian who shares in the divine life received from the Holy Spirit (and which theology calls "sanctifying grace") becomes an adopted son of God, and share the very life of the Holy Trinity. Thus the divine Persons abide in the same "home" with him, and he can always live with them, enjoying their loving company.

Such an intimate sanctifying presence is a mutual presence among persons; an interpersonal relationship between the Christian and the Holy Trinity. The Christian responds to the divine Persons in an extremely personal way. The infusion of divine life into his spirit by the Holy Spirit has made him capable of just such a response. Above all, his is the response of faith, hope and charity, called theological virtues because they do enable the Christian to attain directly to the divine Persons in their inner mystery and without the mediation of any creatures. The theological virtues, particularly charity, experience, "touch," and "taste" the sanctifying presence of the divine Persons every time they produce their acts. By power of the shared divine life, i.e., the sanctifying grace from which they stem, they can, so to speak, take the Christian right into the very intimacy of the Holy Trinity.

The divine Persons come to abide within the Christian when the Holy Spirit grants a share in divine life. The Christian receives that gift of divine life together with the capacity to reciprocate, to reach out and even to enjoy the indwelling presence of these divine Guests. The divine Persons come to the Christian not only to bring their gifts, but to bring themselves. They are loving Givers of a new power to love, enabling the Christian to welcome and embrace them with acts of faith, hope and charity. In addition, even when the theological virtues are not operating with awareness, the indwelling presence of the divine Persons continues without interruption. The divine Persons always remain close at hand in the sanctified Christian. He or she can at any time elicit acts of faith, hope and charity which have the marvelous power to directly attain these same Persons. It is like sitting in a dark room in the presence of a beloved friend: The friend cannot be seen, but he is really there, and one can always stretch out one's hand and touch him, feeling and enjoying his unseen presence.

The *active power* of the theological virtues to reach out and touch the divine Persons abiding in the Christian is actually a participation in the same Persons' power of intimately knowing and loving themselves. But when the Holy Spirit shares with human beings the divine capacity for knowing and loving Them personally, it is inevitably necessary to "adjust" this capacity to our human way of acting. In so doing, such a capacity is weakened. This is why Thomistic theology tried to work out a better explanation of the divine indwelling in Christians by recourse to its characteristic teaching on the seven gifts of the Holy Spirit.

Gifts of the Holy Spirit

These very special "gifts" are conceived as supernatural habitual dispositions. They enable a person to be moved by the operation of the Holy Spirit in order to elicit acts of knowledge and love of God in a way which oversteps the human limits of the acts of the theological virtues. To clarify this distinction, the gifts of the Holy Spirit are compared to the sails of a ship which catch the blowing winds (of the Holy Spirit). Without the human effort of rowing (acts of the theological virtues) they can carry the ship to harbor (into the personal, intimate encounter with the divine Persons abiding within the Christian).

While the rowing attributed to the "theological virtues" remains proportionate to a human and limited way of acting, catching the wind of the Spirit exceeds such limitations. This is true because the "wind of the Spirit" (typical of the "gifts") is actually the human reception of that infinite capacity of knowing and loving proper to the divine Persons themselves.

Both the theological virtues and the gifts of the Holy Spirit are divinely-given capacities assisting one another to *actively* reach out (in the case of the theological virtues) and *receptively* attain (in the case of the gifts of the Holy Spirit) the divine Persons. These divine Guests, while abiding within the Christian as in their own home, offer themselves to his supernatural knowledge and love in all intimacy and immediacy.

The divine Persons' presence within the very being and life of the Christian sanctified by the Holy Spirit is a magnificent privilege. It singles out the Christian and greatly ennobles his individual condition. It makes him the main figure in a very personal, intimate and direct encounter with the Holy Trinity.

Implications for Christian Prayer

Every Christian prayer and mystical experience of the Triune God, must be founded on these supernatural capacities given by the Holy Spirit. They alone enable the Christian to attain to the presence of the divine Persons abiding within. All prayerful Christians have in the virtues and gifts analyzed by Thomistic theology two sets of infused potentialities. Christians can "exercise" themselves by reaching out to the sanctifying presence of the divine Persons through acts of the theological virtues which involve their total human capacity to know and love. They can also "experience" the same presence of these divine Guests by surrendering their human capacity to know and to love to the promptings of the Holy Spirit. Such docile surrender carries them strongly and sweetly into the circulation of life which binds the divine Persons to one another.

This wonderful mystery of the Holy Trinity dwelling within a human person sanctified by the Holy Spirit (with all the virtues and gifts that such sanctification involves) is the foundation of any prayerful or mystical encounter with God. Such prayer enables a Christian to prepare for and experience God. In this way, Christian prayer gives marvelous satisfaction and a sense of achievement to man's deep-rooted human needs and yearnings for the companionship of ever-present and ever-loving, caring friends. No better, more loving, more caring, or more consoling friends could a human being desire than the divine Persons of the Holy Trinity who make their home within him.

PART II
HERMENEUTICS AND PSYCHOLOGY OF PRAYER

CHAPTER 4

BASIC HUMAN, EXISTENTIAL NEEDS, CONTEMPORARY MAN'S ATTITUDES, AND CHRISTIAN PRAYER

Dealing with the themes in the previous chapters, we followed the methods of biblical and theoretical theology. Now we wish to change our perspective, and apply to our subject the "hermeneutical method." This new approach can be explained as follows: the exegetical and theoretical methods of traditional theology take the "Word of God" (*Bible*, Tradition, Magisterium) as their starting-point. Theologians attempt to clarify and to make relevant the revealed content and saving demands of the "Word of God" in order to induce the Christian to respond with full awareness and obedience. The hermeneutical method starts with the human person, or better, with the "human condition or existence" which can be considered in itself and/or in the peculiar shape it takes within the context of contemporary civilization. The final aim here is to discover the needs or repugnances, aptitudes or inabilities, man has in relation to God. Such attitudes call for enlightenment and assistance from the Word of God.

In this way, the hermeneutical method seeks to manifest the actual relevance of God's Word in contemporary human existence.

Following the typical procedure of hermeneutics, we intend to tackle two questions in the present chapter: How can Christian prayer meet man's basic existential needs? What are contemporary man's attitudes towards Christian prayer?

Meaning, Purpose, Companionship

Among the main existential needs which stem from the very essence of man, and are therefore characteristic of the human condition in every time and place, society and culture, the needs for *meaning, purpose* and *companionship* seem to be primary and most commonly experienced. These needs identify so fully with the human person that their satisfaction is practically equivalent to the actual recognition and support of a man's worth and dignity. To help a human person find and develop meaning, purpose and companionship in life is equivalent to acknowledging, appreciating and encouraging his intellectual growth, freedom and ability to communicate with his fellowmen. Intelligence, freedom and communication with others make up the best part of a human being's personality, and contribute to the fulfillment of his existence. They determine the existential "quality" of his life. Human intelligence is always searching for truth, especially for the fundamental truths which give meaning to life. Human free will is oriented to every good which can be creatively pursued throughout life. The unique preciousness of every individual finds security in the acknowledgment, appreciation and love found only in the company of friends. In order to be fully dignified and satisfying, human existence needs to be: enlightened and inspired by true meaning; sustained and energized by valuable purposes; and gladdened by the loving companionship of others. The satisfaction of such basic existential needs decisively gives man reasons and motivations for living, hoping and loving.

Meaning

Since he is a "rational animal," man needs to know what happens or what is going on in his life, and *why*. He desperately needs to lead a life which makes sense to him — and in a way he can consciously grasp. He needs a meaningful life. Only when he grasps the meaning of his existence, and when he is certain that it is a significant one, does the human person feel he is the main figure, and, to some extent, the director in his own life's performance.

When man holds fast to a fundamental existential meaning, and is committed to living in accord with it, he will not be upset or "scandalized" by the apparent obscurities and uncertainties of daily life. Even though they may cause some disturbance and stress, man possesses a clarity and security of mind which enable him to endure and pass through distress without losing his basic steadfastness and determination.

For a human person to feel that he is just dragging along in a meaningless existence is one of the most dreadful of human experiences. Man's natural eagerness for truth, and particularly for existential meaning, is in this case totally frustrated. The human being who identifies so strongly with his search for meaning is crushed and stifled under an existential anguish caused by the conviction of being just a meaningless "thing"; a puppet in the hands of an obscure and cruel fate.

Purpose

Since man is a "rational animal," he is also a "purposeful being." In addition to need for meaning, man also seeks to have a goal. Just as *meaning* satisfies his fundamental need for truth, knowledge and conscious awareness, so *purpose* meets his desire for steering his actions, and eventually his life, towards goals freely chosen by his own will. Not only does his existence need to make sense, but man's activity and sense of commitment must be *purposeful* if he is to feel constructive, creative, self-expressive and self-fulfilling. Every man thinks in terms of expressing and fulfilling himself when he can strive for and purposefully attain his own goals.

But when man is compelled to act and live for no known purpose, or for a purpose which he does not consider worthy of himself, then the activity of his human existence seems to be a mere waste of time. He seems to be senselessly wearing down his energy and life without reason or results. In such a condition, the human person feels deeply depressed and crippled at the very core of his being. Undoubtedly a man who could not find and pursue his own purpose and goals throughout life would eventually end up living an "alienated existence." He would have the humiliating impression of being used; of being merely an instrument for other people's purposes which are then imposed upon him under compulsion and violence.

Companionship

Finally, man is a "social animal." Meaning answers the question *why?* Purpose answers the question *what for?* But another existential demand besides the *why-of-*

living and the *what-for-of-life* must be answered if a person is to reach a fully satisfactory human existence. It is the question of *for whom* one should live?

The last question presupposes and combines both former ones, and enriches them by adding an interpersonal dimension. It is quite evident that man, in addition to meaning and purpose, needs the *company* of other people. It seems that existential meanings and purposes can suffice to give man the foundation of his personal identity, and begin the fulfillment of his growth as a rational and purposeful being, but the actual fulfillment of such growth requires a further acknowledgment, appreciation, concern and support which only other people can give. Man desperately needs to be fully accepted, esteemed, and loved as a *unique person*, and to experience his personal identity insofar as it represents a great value in itself, and in respect to everyone else.

A human being cannot enjoy and develop his existential and personal identity in total isolation from other people, any more than other living beings can thrive in an unfavorable environment. In such a situation they would be exposed to wither and die. Man needs companionship, i.e., people who by their appreciative concern and loving care create around him the necessary spiritual environment favoring the actualization, growth and eventual fulfillment of his personal existence and identity. Indifference, disregard and contempt from other people hurt man's self-esteem and infringe upon his true human dignity, sometimes so seriously as to induce in him the conviction that he is worthless—a thing of no value.

Human existence becomes worth living only when its basic needs for meaning, purpose and companionship are adequately met and sufficiently satisfied. However, a human person needs some kind of meaning, purpose and companionship not only here and now—for the present moment or for the immediate occasions of his existence. He yearns far more for that *ultimate* meaning, purpose and companionship which can impart fundamental existential value upon all the partial meaning, purpose and fellowship of terrestrial life.

Single moments of human life acquire an existential *value* which surpasses the usual triviality characterizing them only if they are lived within the context of an all-pervading life-view and project. This occurs because something existentially *ultimate* is necessarily included within such a context. In this case, even the most trivial moments of human life become meaningful as they are lived within the larger "whole" of man's total life-view and project.

Man's ultimate *meaning* identifies with his life-view, just as his ultimate *purpose* makes up his whole life-project. Only *ultimate companionship* can assure steadfast support to his personal identity. In the last analysis, all this finality in meaning, purpose and companionship originate and are found *only* in the Ultimate Being who is God. It is he who gives ultimate meaning, ultimate purpose and ultimate companionship. Thus, the Christian religion has a specific contribution to make in explaining, and at the same time, in helping man to open up to the human reception of existential finality from God himself:

> Since it has been entrusted to the Church to reveal the mystery of God, who is the ultimate goal of man, she opens up to men at the same time the *meaning of his own existence*, that is, the innermost truth about himself. The Church truly knows that only God, whom she serves, meets the deepest longing of the human heart. . . For man always yearns to know, at least in an obscure way, what is the meaning of his life,

of his activity, of his death. But only God who created man to his own image and ransomed him from sin provides a fully adequate answer to these questions (*Gaudium et Spes* #41).

The traditional teaching on the theological virtues unfolds this "fully adequate response" on the part of the Christian religion to the human existential needs and longings of man for ultimate meaning, purpose and companionship. Faith, hope and charity are called "theological" virtues because they are conceived as supernatural abilities infused by God in order to give man the power to reach out *immediately* (without any mediation of creatures) to the Holy Trinity through knowledge and love. Although all the theological virtues have the entire Trinity as their own specific "object," each divine Person shows some particular likeness to the specific character of one or other of these virtues. Such likeness, when it is considered against the background of the three existential needs we mentioned above, allows for the following statements:

By theological *faith*, the Christian attains God-Truth, who is personified by Jesus Christ, the Incarnate Son of God, and who, as "the Teacher," gives ultimate meaning to the whole of human existence. By theological *hope*, the Christian attains God-Might and Mercy, who can be identified with the Father Almighty, and who, as "the Helper," makes possible the attainment of man's ultimate purpose. By the theological virtue of *charity*, the Christian can reach out after God-Love, who, as the Holy Spirit, is "the Lover" offering man ultimate companionship. Accordingly, the Christian receives a plentiful and wonderful satisfaction of his basic existential needs from the divine Persons themselves through the theological virtues. They truly enable him to live on this earth the life of an adopted child of God.

However, the connection between the divine Persons and the theological virtues is only an approximate insight into the mysterious meeting between the Christian and the Holy Trinity. A more Christocentric approach to the same question can show equivalently that a Christian can find in the multi-faceted personality of Jesus Christ the ultimate satisfaction of his existential needs for meaning, purpose and companionship. Obviously, the following considerations do not represent a retraction of the ones made previously. For in and through Christ we have access to that circulation of life which binds together the three Persons of the Holy Trinity.

Christocentric Approach

Throughout the entire *Bible*, from "Genesis" to "Revelation," God reveals his mystery to man and intervenes by his "Word" in human history itself. This "Word" is already in the Old Testament both "Word-Truth" and "Wisdom"; "Word-Event" and "Might." In the New Testament, the "Word became flesh and dwelt among us," i.e., entered into human history as a Person through Jesus Christ, the only Son of God. Thus, Jesus summarizes and perfects in himself the divine Wisdom expressed by the "Word-Truth" and the saving Might of God actualized by the "Word-Event." Perhaps an example taken from prayer itself may help to clarify this point. We might call out in prayer,

"Jesus, Lord and God, I believe in You!" = You give
    ultimate meaning to my being = faith.
"Jesus, Lord and God, I hope in You!" = All my actions

tend toward the day of ultimate, total union
with You = hope.
"Jesus, Lord and God, I love You!" = You are my
heart's desire and only Your Love can satisfy
that desire = charity.

Clearly, all three theological virtues can find in Jesus their
appropriate and specifically divine "object." Christian
faith is the full personal acceptance of Christ Jesus as the
personified Word-Truth of God. Christian hope is the
trustful relying upon Jesus as the central Word-Event of
redemptive history. Christian charity is the loving
encounter with Christ as the loving Word-Person worthy
of man's return of love and adoration. Thus the
theological virtues can attain through Christ the divine
truth, might and love. Although these divine attributes
may be particularly attributed to each single Person of the
Holy Trinity, properly speaking, they belong to the Holy
Trinity as One, or as a "Unit."
    Against this background we can now ask: how does
Christian prayer meet and satisfy the basic existential
needs of man?

Christian Prayer in Itself

    As a general rule, prayer is the act and attitude of
religion. Together with the acts of sacrifice, it makes up
the core of religious worship. Of course, Christian prayer
can also be considered as a *part* of religious worship. But
that great intimacy with his God which a Christian attains
through the theological virtues turns his prayer into a
direct and immediate meeting and contact with Him in
knowledge, trust and love. For this reason, Christian

prayer is much more than a worshipful expression of natural religion. The specific character of Christian prayer is constituted by theological faith, hope and charity put into action. In fact, the "awareness" we emphasized in our definition of prayer, and the presence of God which fills the Christian's awareness in prayer, are both made possible and actualized by the theological virtues infused by the Holy Spirit. St. Augustine clearly expressed this truth: "In faith, hope and charity themselves we pray always with a constant desire. Consequently, faith and hope and charity lead to God him who prays, i.e., the believing, the hoping, the desiring Christian" (*Epistula ad Probam*, 130, CSEL 44, 57-60).

It should be noted that St. Augustine calls the act of charity "desire" i.e., the love of something not fully attained. God is already present within the Christian, but he will be attained perfectly only in heaven. On earth, our love of him still "walks" in the darkness of faith, and in the distance of hope—which qualify it as "desire." St. Augustine himself explains that our prayer identifies itself with the constant longing for heavenly life: "We always desire the blissful life from God our Lord, and so we pray always" (*Ibid.*).

Every moment of this "theological" prayer brings to the Christian from God the divine certitude of faith, the divine security of hope, and the divine consolation of charity. Such prayer ultimately receives in the presence of God, fully enjoyed, every fulfillment of existential meaning, purpose and companionship. Thus Christian prayer puts into action at one and the same time the most eager human search for those ultimate values, and the most effective discovery and assimilation of them—both of which are so necessary in human life. The well-known words of Jesus on prayer are very much to the point here:

Ask, and it will be given to you; search and you shall
find; knock, and the door will be opened to you. For
the one who asks always receives; the one who
searches always finds; the one who knocks will
always have the door opened to him. . . If you who
are evil know how to give your children what is
good, how much more will the heavenly Father give
the Holy Spirit to those who ask him! (Lk 11:9-13).

Is it not this promised Holy Spirit, the "Spirit of Truth,"
the "Comforter," the "Lover," who grants through his
abiding presence within us the ultimate meaning, purpose
and companionship our earthly existence desperately
needs and ever yearns for? And the Holy Spirit brings
with him the Father and the Son to dwell in our spirit.

Remembering the various "attributions" of the
creative presence of the Father, the saving presence of the
Son, and the sanctifying presence of the Holy Spirit
elaborated upon in the previous chapter, and keeping in
mind the doctrine of the theological virtues developed
here, we can now summarize all our speculations in a
more complete definition of Christian prayer. Our
investigations show quite clearly how such a complex
exercise and experience can communicate to the whole of
human existence life's ultimate meaning, purpose and
companionship received through faith, hope and charity
from the Persons of the Holy Trinity. Hence we can say:
*Christian Prayer is the meaningful believing, the
purposeful hoping, and the companionable loving
awareness of God's creative, saving, and sanctifying
presence within the Christian.*

Obviously, each word of this "concentrated" definition has its own specific significance which ought not to
be missed by anyone who wants to grasp at least the most

important aspects of the multi-faceted mystery of Christian prayer.

Contemporary Mentality and Characteristics

The basic existential needs we have considered are deeply rooted in essential faculties and qualities of human nature (intellect, will, sociability) and remain substantially unchanged in whatever time or place man exists and acts. However, at a more superficial level of experience, we find a great many different mentalities and human characteristics which are formed and conditioned by the society and culture in which man lives.

In actual existence these mentalities and characteristics always affect the concrete display of man's basic existential needs. They help or hinder especially with respect to their ultimate satisfaction in God. To complete in some way our study of man's active predispositions and demands for Christian prayer, we now wish to turn our attention to the average mentality and character of contemporary man in relation to Christian prayer. We can only suppose that some traits of contemporary mentality and character may be favorable and conducive to Christian prayer, while others seem more unfavorable and detrimental to it.

Against the background of our general definition of prayer (loving awareness of God's presence), it is evident that every aspect of the mentality and character of contemporary man which helps or hinders him in detecting and perceiving the "signs" of God's presence in the world and among men are also gains or losses for the act of Christian prayer. We wish to emphasize that :

—in particular, an over-all technological and

pragmatic frame of mind causes the inhabitants of our cities to drift far from the "signs" of God's creative presence in the universe. And thus, even though such "signs" may not be totally obliterated, they appear quite blurred to the eyes of contemporary man.

—on the other hand, the "signs" of God's saving presence in *human history* seem to have gained today in visibility and relevance.

—although such "signs" may exist, it must be noted that contemporary man's characteristic bent toward a better future attained through *human* effort risks causing these "signs" to fade away as symbols of *God's* saving presence in human history.

Let us now develop in detail each one of these points. In describing the "changing conditions of human life," Vatican II expressed some judgments which still hold true:

> Intellectual formation is ever increasingly based on the mathematical and natural sciences and on those dealing with man himself, while in the practical order the technology which stems from these sciences takes on mounting importance. This *scientific spirit* exerts a new kind of impact on the cultural sphere and on modes of thought (*Gaudium et Spes*, #5).

> Unlike former days, the denial of God and religion, or the abandonment of them, are no longer unusual and individual occurrences. For today, it is not rare for such a decision to be presented as *requirements of scientific progress* or of a certain new humanism (*GS.*, #7).

An imbalance arises between a concern for *practicality and efficiency,* and the demands of a moral conscience; also, very often between the conditions of collective existence and the requisite of personal thought, and even of contemplation (*GS.,* #8).

Modern civilization itself often complicates the approach to God, not for any essential reason, but because it is *excessively engrossed in earthly affairs* (*GS.,* #19).

Wisdom and the Gifts of the Holy Spirit

What has been said, of course, puts the matter discussed not in lesser but greater need of wisdom and the "gift of the Spirit."

The intellectual nature of the human person is perfected by wisdom, and it needs to be. For wisdom greatly attracts the mind of man to a quest and a love for what is true and good. *Steeped in wisdom, man passes through visible realities to those that are unseen.* Our era needs such wisdom more than bygone ages if the discoveries made by man are to be further humanized. For the future of the world stands in peril unless wiser men are forthcoming. . . It is finally *through the gift of the Holy Spirit that man comes by faith to the contemplation and appreciation of the divine plan* (*GS.,* #15).

As an explanatory note on these authoritative insights of Vatican II, we wish to note that sheer technology seems to wither the flower of poetry, just as pragmatism tends to exclude metaphysics. Only a certain amount of poetical imagination and a metaphysical frame of mind can lay open the human spirit to the mystery of God the Creator, and make man sensitive to his creative presence in the world. Poetry uses imaginative symbols as stepping-stones to attain God's mysterious presence, while metaphysics has at its disposal analogical concepts which enable man to make the same discovery. Technology replaces poetical images taken from nature as created by God with testimonies of man's creativity and power: i.e., man-made products and machines. Pragmatism, on its part, rejects any metaphysical knowledge of the world which could lift the human mind from creatures to God. Pragmatism is interested only in a utilitarian knowledge of the world, pursued for the practical purpose of obtaining and spreading man's dominion over this world. Accordingly, the usual psychological "roads" leading to the discovery of God's presence seem blocked off to the average citizen of our technological and practical society.

"Secularization and Celebration"

This cultural phenomenon has been called the "secularization of the modern world." Contemporary man, who is under the intellectual, psychological and moral pressures of "secularization," tends to acquire an exclusively materialistic and positivistic approach to the world, and then we have pure "secularism." He tends to develop a totally "secularized" thought-pattern and language, which describe and interpret human experience in merely "secularized" terms (i.e., materialistic, pragmatic, scientific and technological) so that there is no room left for any insightful human sensitivity to God's creative presence in the world. Instead of believing—as the Christian does—that a loving, caring, creative presence of God permeates the universe and embraces all men, the "secularized" citizen of our technological cities looks at the world as at an immense empty fabric dominated by utter indifference towards mankind. The typical religious admiration and awe before God's mysterious yet powerful creative presence in the world is replaced by "secularized" man's tragic sense of loneliness and despair before an immense and empty universe.

An overall reaction against our "secularized" civilization has recently given birth to a renewed poetical approach to nature, and to a more playful or festive approach to human life. Prayer and celebration have had a revival—especially among the younger generation—with the new cultural emphasis on leisure and festivity. People today *have* become capable once again of perceiving God's presence in their lives and in the world. Even though a metaphysical approach to God's presence may be more difficult for modern man, quite a few theologians (e.g., Paul Tillich, L. Gilskey and others) think that an objective ontology is still needed for a better understanding of man's life, destiny, and relations with God. We wish to add that it is needed also for becoming prayerfully aware of God's creative, conservative and progressive presence in the universe.

God's Presence in Society and in History

While the "signs" of God's creative presence in our world seem to be outshone by man's powerful technology, which "is now transforming the face of the earth, and is already trying to master outer space" (*GS.,* #5) other "signs" of God's saving presence in human society and history are beginning to appear and be perceived by contemporary man. Human sensitivity for such "signs" has increased in our historically and socially-oriented civilization. In fact, today it can said that:

to a certain extent, the human intellect is broadening its dominion over time: over the past by means of *historical knowledge*; over the future by the art of *projecting and by planning.* Advances in biology, psychology, and the social sciences not only bring men hope of improved self-knowledge, but in conjunction with technical methods, they are also helping men to *exert direct influence on the life of social groups* (*GS.,* #3).

Thus, contemporary man's discovery and awareness of God's presence does not follow, as it did in the past, the path traced through his own interior life. Rather, man today chooses an outward road, passing through human society and history. Actually, contemporary man is convinced that salvation must occur within human history and society, and not just within individual souls. Accordingly, the Catholic Church today also emphasizes the fulfillment of God's saving power through the social events of human history.

Such saving historical events have been called "signs of the times" by John XXIII and by Vatican Council II (cf. *GS.,* #4):

The People of God believes that it is led by the Spirit of the Lord, who fills the earth. Motivated by this faith, it labors to decipher *authentic signs of God's presence* and purpose in the happenings, needs, and desires in which this People has a part along with other men of our age. For faith throws a new light on everything, manifests God's designs for man's total vocation, and thus directs the mind to solutions which are fully human (*GS.*, #11).

Evidently this passage was written on the assumption that *not all* events, needs and desires of contemporary men are authentic signs of God's saving presence. The People of God needs, therefore, to discern their meaning in the light of faith granted by the Spirit of the Lord. The People of God—and not each individual Christian—has the assurance of the Holy Spirit's assistance in scrutinizing and interpreting those "signs" against the background of God's redemptive history. After all, God's People, the Church herself, is a privileged "event and sign" of his saving presence among men within human history. On the one hand, since the Church is the "Body of Christ," She is the earthly extension of the Incarnate Son of God, Jesus Christ, who is THE Savior, i.e., the chief and personified "Event" of divine saving presence within human history. On the other hand, the Holy Spirit abides in the Church in order to bring the whole of mankind to final salvation through her.

Coming forth from the eternal Father's love, founded in time by Christ the Redeemer, and made one in the Holy Spirit (Ep 1:8; 5:6, 13-14, 23), the Church has a saving and eschatological purpose which can be fully attained only in the future world. But she is already present in the world, and is composed of men, that is, of members of the earthly city who have a call to form the family of God's children during the present history of the human race, and to keep increasing it until the Lord returns (*GS.*, #40).

What happens in the world needs to be scrutinized and discerned as a possible event of salvation in the light of that privileged event which is constituted by Jesus Christ and the Holy Trinity, present and savingly active in the Church. Needless to say, God's saving presence at work in world history cannot contradict God's saving presence at work in the Church. If historical events contradict salvation events, then it is clear that what is operating in the events of human history cannot be a "sign" of God's saving presence at all.

Faith and Discernment

The role assigned to faith, i.e., the adhesion of man to the full mystery of salvation, is of great importance in scrutinizing and deciphering the "signs of the times." This role emphasizes that *only* through a living faith cultivated by the Christian community, is it possible to detect the authentic saving presence of God mysteriously at work in human history and throughout the world. The other theological virtues whose first foundation is given by faith are certainly associated with faith. Christian awareness of God's presence can only be given by the theological virtues, and since this awareness is the very essence of Christian prayer, it follows that discerning the authentic "signs of the times" in historical events can be successful only when carried out with a fervent spirit of Christian prayer. Such a spirit constitutes that supernatural sensitivity which is absolutely required to perceive God's presence beyond the worldly appearances of human events. Only when Christians enliven their involvement in social history with a fervent spirit of faith leading into prayer and contemplation, can they attain that insight of prophetic wisdom which enables them to discern God's presence at work in the events, needs and desires of contemporary mankind.

The spirit of Christian prayer is perfectly suited to the socially and historically-oriented mentality of our times. This spirit contributes divine depth to such a mentality, without in any way diminishing its keen insight into all concrete cultural circumstances of human existence. Those circumstances are usually called "events," namely, something "happening" to individuals and groups within human society and history. The spiritual content of events is given by the persons involved in them. Such persons qualify the events with their personal presence, while the events themselves may be compared to a "cocoon" or the environment enfolding these persons.

When getting in touch with an event, one may discover a spiritual, personal presence. Christianity is a religion substantially made up of a constant progression of saving historical events, wherein God's presence reveals itself more and more powerfully among men. Faith, hope and charity create in Christians that insightful awareness of the historical events of salvation. Such prayerful awareness penetrates Christians so deeply as to reveal God's presence at work in and through them for the spreading of salvation among all men.

Within the framework of redemptive history where human events assume the character of "signs of the times," they can be changed into good opportunities for the awakening of a Christian's theological awareness of God's saving presence. They can nourish Christian prayer even through the turmoil of human society and history. In those events which faith deciphers as authentic "signs of the times," Jesus Christ himself is mysteriously at work as our *Savior*, who meets all men, but especially Christians, in order to sanctify them. Prayer's believing, hoping and loving awareness of and attention to the coming of God,

Savior and Lord, is the most appropriate response Christians can make to the presence of Jesus Christ in the happenings of human society and history.

Obstacles to Discernment

But the socio-historical mentality of contemporary man does not always assist the discovery of God's saving presence in human events. Quite a few of our fellowmen, as far as their socio-historical tendency is concerned, envision a better future which, in their opinion, will be the result of human efforts alone. The socio-economic conditions of present-day industrial society may have been a decisive factor in the birth and development of this future-oriented man-made project. For instance, the great mobility of our society gives the impression that we will be quickly taken by the stream of evolution into a proximate future, totally different from our present setup; and the continual growth in the production of commodities increases the desire for greater affluence available to all in a short space of time.

Hence, ideologies which favor the future and emphasize an evolutionary optimistic view of the world have been elaborated. The nature of man has been conceived as a "bundle of possibilities" lacking only sufficient opportunity to be put effectively into action within a social effort for man's earthly betterment. Such recent philosophies of man and the world are fundamentally atheistic. They affirm that man is capable of saving himself in a better future without any need of God's saving intervention in human history. Some schools of Christian theology have, during the last decade, tried to "ransom" these ideologies and insert them within the Christian conception of God's redemptive activity in the world. This is the way in which "Political Theology," the "Theology of Hope," "Theology of Liberation," and others, have originated.

"Christian Future," "Christian Present"

Christianity has an essential orientation towards the future. In theological terminology it is called the "eschatological dimension" of the Kingdom of God. But the "future" at which Christianity aims represents an "absolutely better" existence granted by God alone to mankind. Faith teaches that God's Kingdom, whose perfect fulfillment is to be awaited in a meta-historical future, is already at work in the *present time.* It is present as a mystery of God's salvation hidden within human society and history.

We do not exclude a human thrust towards a better future, both human and divine; historical and meta-historical. Such a drive stems inevitably from the actual deepening of the prayerful awareness of God's saving presence. That awareness represents for the Christian the living seed of his socio-historical commitment to a better future. It is sown in his soul by his very encounter with God's presence; the God who operates within human history! With such awareness, the Christian receives a foretaste of the unveiled eschatological meeting with his God beyond time and history. Such a "foretaste" greatly sharpens his desire to enjoy God's presence after the fulfillment of his commitment in this life.

Contemporary man needs more than what the various new ideologies of hope and liberation offer. These may take care of his flight towards a better historical future, but man also needs to be assisted in becoming aware of God's saving presence abiding in the depths of his *present* experience. Too much emphasis on the future can easily become an escape from the present, through daydreaming and wishful thinking. Such an unrealistic attitude misses the only one concrete opportunity real existence offers to man and to the Christian here and now. The new notions of hope and liberation could become escapes from facing God's presence *now*, in and through Christian prayer. They could tend toward a pretentious and supposedly more perfect encounter with Him in the midst of future-oriented socio-historical action. On the contrary, a solid theology and spirituality of Christian prayer, rooted in hope, faith, and charity, is more complete than any unilateral theology of hope or liberation, and reminds the Christian of his "contemporaneity" with Jesus Christ who is already at work as Saving Lord at every moment of human history.

CHAPTER 5

A THEOLOGICAL PSYCHOLOGY OF CHRISTIAN PRAYER

Now we turn our attention in a more direct and analytical manner to the psychology of prayer, which is a complex and multi-faceted psychological phenomenon involving all inner faculties of human free activity. From the psychological viewpoint, prayer can be described broadly as a conversation or dialogue between God and man, characterized by exercise and experience.

Now we wish to develop several new considerations, taking the concepts of conversation, exercise and experience as guidelines to the psychological foundation and content of Christian prayer. This psychology of prayer will not be the research of a behavioral science. Rather, it will be a systematic reflection developed against the background of the mystery of God, of man, and of man's divinely-infused faculties activated by Christian prayer. We call our psychology of prayer "theological."

A very common psychological description of prayer presents it as *conversation* or dialogue between man and God. By such a description, one evidently wishes to emphasize the particular mutuality or relation of reciprocity prayer effects between God and man. Within such a framework, several characteristics of Christian prayer may be noted: its mysteriousness; its being centered in God's Word; its dialectical pattern; its extraordinary intimacy.

Mysteriousness of Christian Prayer

A "mystery" is something which is beyond comprehension, because it lies beyond the range of human understanding. Why do we say that prayer, especially Christian prayer, and precisely insofar as it is a phenomenon of human psychology, is a "mystery?" Well, prayer as conversation can be compared to the sparks produced within an electric field. Both poles producing the sparks of Christian prayer are a "mystery of faith."

On one side we find man, created in God's image, restored by Christ as an adopted son of God, and indwelt by the Holy Spirit. This is, as it were, the "negative pole." For, from the image of God imprinted in his very being, from his divine sonship, and from the indwelling presence of the Holy Spirit, there wells up within the Christian heart a "Godward" thrust toward conversation with Jesus Christ and with the Persons of the Holy Trinity. Herein lies the very essence of Christian prayer. Theology explains that the image of God in man is ontologically related to its exemplary cause and dynamically oriented towards it. Man, by his very nature, is *capax Dei* ("capable of God"), and is driven by an unquenchable natural desire for attaining God and conversing with him. Even though his merely natural power is not able to reach out to encompass God, man is still restless until he does meet God. Divine adoption and the infusion of the Holy Spirit give man precisely that real possibility and a beginning of such attainment. Christian prayer turns it into a free and conscious intimacy.

The other pole, the "positive one" by which Christian prayer is enkindled, is God himself. He comes to meet man's Godwards thrust by granting him his divine presence. God acts in prayer like a magnet drawing filings to itself: all human beings. He who creates in the human heart a hunger for God also satisfies that need by making Himself accessible and present to the Christian in prayer.

Both poles from which Christian prayer as conversation issues are "mysteries of faith." Consequently, Christian prayer in its very core is a "mystery," although it may occur and manifest itself within the realm of psychology. Due to its essential mysteriousness, A. Stolz has emphasized the "meta-psychological" character of Christian prayer. The psychological experience which a Christian can have of his prayer as conversation with God is only the tip of a deep iceberg—representing his intimate and unexpressed communion of life with Him.

Prayer Centered in God's Word

Christian prayer is quite appropriately, although analogically, called "conversation" because it displays an imperfect but real similarity to the usual way in which human beings speak with one another. In fact, words are the main means people use to communicate. Such understanding of Christian prayer can be found throughout the *Bible*, which lays so much stress on the fact that God comes among men and addresses Himself to them by His "Word" of revelation. Christian prayer finds its center and pivot in God's Word! It is only in *God's* language that we can commune with Him.

"When you pray, you address yourself to the Bridegroom (Jesus Christ); when you read (Holy

Scripture), he speaks to you," wrote St. Jerome to the Christian virgin Eustochium (*Letters*, n 22, 25, PL 22, 411; cf also St. Augustine, *Enarrationes in Psalmos*, 85, n 5, PL 37,1086: "Your prayer is conversation with God: when you read, God speaks to you; when you pray, you speak to God;" Also St. Ambrose, *De Officiis ministrorum*, L.I., c 20, n 88, PL 16, 50).

The Christian can address himself to God in prayer only because *God first* addresses Himself to him, and invites him to intimate dialogue. In this sense God is always the first to speak. Sometimes the Christian may seem to be the initiator of his conversation with God, but he is only responding to a mysterious "word-call" from God. Actually, the very essence of Christian prayer is the human echoing back to God of God's words, proclaimed publicly or suggested privately to the Christian. Therefore, the official prayers of the Church are for the most part taken from Holy Scripture, which is the revealed Word of God *par excellence*. In truth, we really do not know how to pray; how to address ourselves to God. If he had not come to our aid with his Word to prompt us, we would be absolutely speechless before him (Rm 8:26-27). Yet God has been so good that he not only speaks to us with his Word, but he even bestows on us those divinely infused faculties by which we are able to receive and answer that Word.

Christian theology teaches that the praying Christian grasps and responds to the manifold content of the divine Word by the theological virtues, reinforced by the contemplative "gifts" of the Holy Spirit. We can summarize this doctrine as follows: the divine *Word-Truth*, which exerts an ultimate meaning-giving power on human existence, is grasped and responded to by the theological virtue of *faith*. And *faith* receives from the "gift" of *intelligence* a special piercing insight. The divine

Word-Event, which exercises an ultimate purpose-giving power on human existence, is received and experienced by the theological virtue of *hope*. Hope is illumined and strengthened by the "gift" of *science*. The divine *Word-Person*, which exerts an eternal life-and-love giving power on human existence, is met and welcomed by the theological virtue of *charity*. The "gift" of *wisdom* contributes to charity an intimate connaturality for knowing and loving God, which is, indeed, a very special "empathy" with God.

The Christian psychology of prayer is a quiet, composed listening to and receiving of God's Word, coupled with a complex human response of obedience, trust and love. It is the Word of God, with its swinging from God to man, and bouncing back from man to God, which creates and manifests the typical dialectical pattern of Christian prayer.

Dialectical Pattern

As far as the partners involved in the dialogue of prayer are concerned, Christian prayer is a "mystery of faith." If we consider the attitude and activity of the praying Christian, we discover that prayer is a "paradox," for it appears to be made up of apparently contradictory elements brought into unity. Prayer does show in action a fundamental dialectical pattern which puts together and sums up both listening and responding, silence and speech, receptivity and activity, poverty and richness.

As in every really mutual conversation, the moment of listening can hardly be overemphasized in prayer. Moreover, since the relation between the Christian and his God is similar to that between an extremely ignorant disciple and his most wise master, the Christian in prayer desperately needs to listen to God! Scripture says: "Speak, Lord, your servant is listening to you!" We always remain poor creatures, even after becoming adopted children of God. All we are and have is given to us beforehand through the initiative of a loving God. Our prayer, too, is a gift from God. Perhaps it is the very last evidence that his mercy is still with us, even when we might have wasted or lost all his other graces.

The proper attitude for fruitful listening in prayer is an inner stillness and silence of the spirit. God the Father speaks only one Word in his eternal silence: it is his beloved Son. Only a silent person can hear it in prayer, as St. John of the Cross teaches. To remain still and silent is a necessary prerequisite for the human spirit's receptivity to God's Word and presence. Man needs to acknowledge his radical poverty before God. He needs to know that all by himself he is just like a dark and figureless mirror devoid of the shining light and face. Through the listening and silence of prayer, the Christian realizes his radical nakedness and his need to remain openly receptive to the self-giving of his God. Nothing more than prayer gives man an insightful knowledge of himself. Prayer brings about that human self-disclosure in the face of God's presence which affords the human person the most perfect knowledge of himself, of his own nothingness in respect of God who is All according to St. Catherine of Siena.

Together with all the listening, silence, poverty and nothingness which compose its "negative" or "passive" side, there is in prayer another aspect which shows a clearly "positive" and "active" character. This unity of apparently opposing sides constitutes what we have called the dialectical pattern or "paradox" of Christian prayer.

Prayer is not only listening to God. The praying man also responds to him, and this response represents the reverse of listening. The response of prayer does have some kinship with listening to God, since it springs forth from the same attention or awareness required for listening to him. From that inner attention flows a full response when the praying man, leaving his receptive attitude of silence, begins to speak to God.

Receptivity then turns into a spiritual activity which can be imagined as the reflection of God's light and face in the human spirit as in a clear and shining mirror. By this reflective answering activity, we gain evidence that some share of the infinite divine richness has permeated the praying person through and through. God's own richness meets and far surpasses man's radical poverty of spirit. In uttering words of prayer, man is like a child who shows by its wise speech just how much he has made his own the instructive words of his father.

Prayer is a complex spiritual phenomenon made up of listening, silence, receptivity, and "poverty" before God. It is completed by the praying man's response, speech, activity and "richness" with respect to him. There is a constant interplay between these two attitudes, so that the seemingly opposite elements of each alternate dialectically with one another. The attitudes of the "passive" side come first and cause the attitudes of the "active" side. As rain and snow falling on the mountains precede and feed the streams of a river, so is the divine influence in the spirit of the praying Christian previous to any response of the latter in relation to God.

Intimacy of Christian Prayer

Before closing our comments on prayer as conversation, we should point out the extraordinary intimacy which characterizes the dialogue of prayer between man and God. When man is really listening to God in prayer, the divine Word and Persons penetrate to the innermost recesses of his spirit. Nothing and no one can speak to the human heart in so penetrating, convincing, and moving a manner as God can. A created person who attempts to enter into the heart of man by gestures, words, the prestige of authority, and love, to a great extent falls short of his expectations in the face of the impenetrable citadel of intimate privacy which belongs exclusively to each individual. One may deliberately close his heart to another person as in the presence of an intruder, or, he may open it wide as to a dear friend. Yet it is the very privacy of the human heart itself which does not permit total self-disclosure to any other created person. Whenever two created persons try to inter-penetrate each other through sincerity and love, they still always remain two distinct finite beings, ontologically separated from one another. But *God* who as Creator of the human heart is "more intimate to man than his very own intimacy" and who constantly watches over man's innermost core of privacy, cannot be hindered from stepping into it to make his home there when man is willing to give him free admittance.

The most interior human privacy is not beyond the range of God's action, and it is not violated, but rather exalted by God who establishes his presence within it. The silent and listening attitude of prayer can lay the heart of man wide open before God with total assurance. Such an attitude allows the piercing efficacy of God's Word and of his saving, sanctifying presence to penetrate the innermost citadel of the human heart. In fact, the heart of a Christian who really prays does not shrink from disclosing his most intimate secrets, for better or for worse, to his God and Father. Such a sincere and devout Christian does not even think of taking anything of his intimate privacy away from God's eyes. Rather, he yearns ardently to be permeated through and through by God's searching and consoling presence. Such total self-disclosure is accompanied by self-surrender which both perfectly actualizes the human fundamental receptivity before God, and also fills with God's richness the radical poverty of the human spirit. Indeed, we can conclude that through prayer, God takes full possession of man's mind and heart.

Such a statement can easily be confirmed by the other acts and attitudes we find on the "active" side of prayer as conversation. What we usually describe as a heart-to-heart talk with a dear friend implies the expression, communication, and in some form, also the dedication of the person who speaks to the one invited to share in the secrets of his heart. Something like this occurs in the Christian's response to God in prayer. Such prayer can be described as the most intimate form of heart-to-heart speech. When the Christian, after listening in silence, begins to speak to God, he certainly expresses and communicates himself to Him as perfectly as possible. His deepest thoughts, feelings, yearnings and desires emerge from the depths of his heart, and manifest themselves to God at the moment of prayer, culminating in self-dedication to God.

The spoken response of prayer is an *expression* of the most intimate thoughts and feelings of one's heart, a *communication* of the most personal secrets of one's life, and an *adoring dedication* of one's very being to God. This is the reason we have attributed an extraordinary depth and intimacy to the conversation between man and God which *is* Christian prayer.

The word "conversation" permits a broad description of prayer as a psychological phenomenon. A more particularized approach to the subject can be given by the concept of *"exercise."* Articulate exercise is required to reach that awareness of God's presence which is of the very essence of prayer. This "ascetic" facet of prayer, from the very first centuries of the Christian era, was described as the "ascent or lifting up of the mind to God." In the following pages we shall analyze the human faculties put into action in the exercise of prayer; the principal goals of that exercise; and the two fundamental forms it takes.

Human Faculties Actualized

Prayer as *exercise* involves the praying man's need to apply his spirit, to make progressive spiritual efforts to attain loving attention to God's presence, and to persevere in these efforts. Prayer usually requires a serious, steady "training" of the spirit in *seeking* God's presence, in *striving* to become aware of it, and in lovingly *keeping* it alive within one's being. In performing this "exercise," the praying man puts into action both his mind and heart (his faculties of attention and affection).

The human *mind* contributes recollection, concentration and meditation, which produce the typical "awareness" of prayer. Intellectual and imaginative (also aesthetical) potentialities are actualized in prayer. Both forms of knowledge are of great use in achieving and sustaining the exercise of prayer.

As far as the aesthetic, imaginative knowledge is concerned, we find in several spiritual masters an intimate union between prayer and poetry (cf. St. John of the Cross). The presence of God which is the proper object of prayer is a supra-human mystery, and cannot be directly known by the human mind. It is characteristic of poetry to use the metaphorical language of images, symbols and similes to give an aesthetic glimpse of realities otherwise scarcely perceived or understood. Hence poetry seems to be suitable for approaching the mystery of God's presence in a manner which can help our awareness of God in prayer.

While the poetical approach uses imaginative symbols, the intellectual insight employs conceptual analogies as a means of attaining to God's mysterious presence. The analogies bear the ideas contained in the metaphors, and the metaphors represent the outward trappings of these ideas. Christian tradition describes the lifting-up of the human mind to God by way of conceptual analogy as follows: starting from the knowledge of creatures, and going back along the path traced by God's creative action, the human mind can figure out several traits of the hidden face of God, Source of all creation. Creatures are always more or less imperfect. But no imperfection can be admitted in God. Hence the human mind must deny to God any of those imperfections it recognizes in creatures. All perfections of creatures must be acknowledged as existing in God, but in an infinitely more extensive and outstanding manner, without limitation. A kind of dazzling contemplation, obtained as the end of this whole itinerary, and received as a pure flash of insightful understanding, takes hold of the human mind when it directly meets—even though dimly—the magnificent perfection and splendor of God in himself.

The human *mind* (intelligence and imagination cooperating with each other) should learn a "technique" of attention, recollection and meditation, or a method of ascension to God which may help one to become aware of his presence. Contemplative prayer brings to completion all human efforts, bringing them to their culmination in a very simple insight which pierces the mystery of God's presence. Such contemplative prayer is not merely an act of the mind. The human *heart*, i.e., the human faculties of love and affection, also makes a very important and necessary contribution to the exercise of prayer: one which involves the *whole person*. The human heart has two levels of affectivity, just as the human mind has two levels of knowledge. The heart's levels are termed emotional sensibility and will. Both concur in opening up and in directing the whole heart of man toward God's presence in prayer.

Sometimes the exercise of prayer can occasion a good deal of sensitive fervor and joy, causing the praying man to experience God's presence in a way that is exciting and gladdening, according to the words of the Psalmist, "Taste and see how sweet is the Lord. . . My heart and my flesh have exulted in the living God" (Ps 34:9, 84:3).

But as far as the *human will* is concerned, the exercise of prayer seems to be identified with an inner effort to comply with the will of God. It is typical of friends to have one will (to will the same thing; to not-will the same thing), as they are one in mutual love. Since Christian prayer is an expression of friendship or, of loving filial submission to God the Father, it demands such conformity. Christ taught us this obedient, compliant prayer to the Father several times during his public life (recall: "Thy will be done on earth as it is in heaven"), and he himself gave the most perfect example of it with his insistent supplication: "Father, if you are willing, remove this cup from me; nevertheless, not my will but yours be done" (Mt 26:39).

Even when sensible fervor is unattainable or has faded away, a prayer of austere conformity and abandonment to the will of God remains possible. Indeed, it is still required of us. It may be the most worthy prayer that we are able to utter at that moment. All spiritual "detachments" which are so necessary to the Christian life are then taken up into the exercise of this "prayer of pure will," which is a will-to-love!

Principal Goals

We can understand why the principal goals of the exercise of prayer can be comprehensively expressed by the word "freedom." The exercise of prayer can be *broadly* conceived as an effort for inner liberation. In the striving for interior freedom which characterizes this exercise, two dimensions are involved: a yearning for the "freedom-from," which is realized by exerting spiritual control over man and his worldly condition; and an earnest desire of the "freedom-for," which is attained when one can undisturbedly apply one's spirit to the presence of God.

The exercise of prayer aims at achieving a sufficient freedom from all humdrum daily occupations and preoccupations, from excessive concern for and attachment to "worldly" affairs, for such concerns divert the Christian from paying attention to God and from giving his affection to Him. This exercise is a challenging "ascetical" dimension of prayer. It is so much needed in prayer that without some form of spiritual detachment and inner recollection, it is practically impossible to pray at all.

It would be useless to strive for inner "freedom-from," if the peace of mind involved in it could not be changed into an opportunity of practising "freedom-*for*" applying, centering, dedicating one's mind and heart to God in and through prayerful awareness of his presence. Such adhesion of the human spirit to God is the most rewarding "mystical" facet of prayer. It was beautifully expressed by the Latin words used during the Middle Ages to describe the contemplative life: *vacare Deo*, which means "to be unemployed," "off-duty," "on vacation," for God.

In its challenging-ascetical dimension, the exercise of prayer, aiming to acquire this inner "freedom-from," is chiefly a man-oriented activity. It is a sort of tidying-up of one's spirit, in order to prepare it to welcome God. It involves the progressive purification of both mind and heart, cutting off by detachment all things which entangle and "glue" man to a worldly way of life. The final result should be the "cleanness" of the human spirit, cleansed as a mirror made ready to receive the splendor of divine light.

But in its rewarding-mystical dimension, the exercise of prayer is clearly God-oriented. The "cleanness" or purity attained during the previous exercise is here applied to God in such a way that it becomes an actual expectation and almost an implicit appeal for his presence—much like the empty hand of a beggar extended to the rich man passing by. Remembering some evangelical similes, we may imagine that the God-oriented exercise of Christian prayer is like knocking at the gate of the city of God and asking to be admitted; or, it is like opening the door of our spirit to the Lord who is always knocking at our door. In such cases, a very intimate meeting and union between the praying Christian and God is equally awaited.

Obstacles to Exercise

In short: prayer as an *exercise*, both of mind and heart, involves a twofold effort of self-disclosure and self-surrender to God. The self-disclosure exhibits the praying man, so to speak, as spiritually "naked" in the sight of God, just as the self-surrender makes him "vulnerable" before God's powerful action. Therefore, in and through the exercise of prayer, one becomes spiritually wide open and given over to God's influence and presence. For the same reason, a Christian can be prevented from engaging in prayer by conscious or unconscious fears of exhibiting his "nakedness" and "vulnerability" to God. Two opposing fears seem to hinder the self-disclosure and self-surrender of man in prayer. There is the fear of not being loved enough by God, and of not being sufficiently enriched by his gifts. After all, we do not appreciate ourselves so much as to think that we are worthy of God's love, and if we really give up our created goods, will we not be destitute of everything? This fear can and ought to be overcome by a Christian through faith in the infinite love and munificence God has for and bestows upon man. As St. John wrote: "We ourselves have known and put our faith in God's love towards ourselves" (1Jn 4:16).

Paradoxically opposed to the previous fear, man can also fear being loved by God in a "possessive" manner, and this we must also consider. We may fear that God's love for us might become more and more demanding, like the love of a jealous lover who wants us totally for himself. How much would we prefer that God left us alone and in our privacy. And so, we exert our "right of self-defense" against him. One can find dramatic examples of this fear and resistance in the lives of Elijah and Jeremiah. Such fear can and should be dispelled by humble confidence in a God who really respects and protects our freedom, willing our true happiness. We need a perfect love of God to attain this fearless self-surrender to him in prayer. For in truth, "In love there can be no fear; because to fear is to expect punishment, and anyone who is afraid is still imperfect in love. We are to love, then, because he loved us first" (1Jn 4:18-19).

Modes of Prayer as Exercise

Prayer as exercise can be carried out in two different ways, and these are as fundamental as the *individual* and the *social* character of the human person. The exercise of prayer can be either private, i.e., personal, or public, i.e., shared, communal, liturgical.

Private prayer is a "need," like hunger and thirst, as well as a "right," like eating and drinking. The need must be satisfied, as the right ought to be respected in such a way that the praying Christian may dedicate himself to this form of prayer in stillness and solitude.

When you pray, go to your private room and, when you have shut the door, pray to your Father Who is in that secret place, and your Father Who sees all that is done in secret will reward you. In your prayer do not babble as the pagans do, for they think that by using many words they will make themselves heard. Do not be like them; your Father knows what you need before you ask him (Mt 6:6-8).

Public prayer is a task and a duty: a worshipful service offered to God out of love within the Christian community, and an example of faith and devotion given to one's brothers and sisters.

Where two or three are united through prayer in my name, I am, says the Lord, in their midst,
                         and
When two or three Christians agree in asking together something of God, it will be granted to them.

This form of public, communal prayer within the Christian community is often associated in one way or another with the sacrifice of Christ, re-enacted in the Eucharistic celebration. In this way it becomes an essential part of liturgical worship; it is itself a "sacrifice of praise" offered to God.

Having quite a distinct character, finality and function for the individual and for the community, these two fundamental forms of Christian prayer also show a different mode of actualization. The private, personal prayer may be absolutely free as far as postures, words and gestures are concerned. It can be so spontaneous and extemporaneous that no fixed pattern is imposed upon it. On the other hand, every public, communal, and especially liturgical prayer must be necessarily vocal, and usually is molded in precise formulas and rites which are neither extemporaneous nor subject to individual inspiration.

Balance and Integration

Sometimes the dissimilar characteristics of these two forms of prayer may be so exaggerated that each of them becomes one-sided. When the first form of prayer, the private one, is esteemed too exclusively, one tends to exaggerate spontaneity, sentimentalism, self-centeredness and individualism. This danger is always threatening man's prayer life. It could be associated with the well-known temptation to "spiritual hedonism," which inclines the praying person to seek for the consolation of God more than for the God of consolation. But when the second form, the communal one, is too exclusively emphasized, the risk of falling into "liturgical ritualism" is a real one. Worship then tends to turn into a merely external rite, celebrated, perhaps, with a perfect observance of all the liturgical rules, but devoid of devotional content. Such merely ritual prayer would be reduced to a fictitious performance, and the praying man to a showman or actor who does not cultivate any loving awareness of God's presence in his prayer.

Both forms of prayer should be integrated with one another just as with the individual and social dimensions of the human person. Generally speaking, every Christian should add some public, communal prayers to his individual, personal ones, and all prayers of the Christian community should be enlivened by the inner devotion of those who offer them. Particularly in communal prayer, individual devotion may be aided by choosing, for example, those common prayer-formulas which are more suited to the mind and sensibility of the participants. However, biblical or scriptural texts should always be privileged, because they contain the words which God himself gave us as a basic food for our prayer.

At this point there arises the problem of whether most Christians are really able to understand a very difficult text of the *Bible*. The Church has always tried to obviate this difficulty by offering to the faithful, especially during the reading of the Holy Scripture, an authorized commentary and commentators. However, to feed his prayer (private and public) with Scriptural reading, a Christian needs that spiritual insight born of faith and love, much more than the scientific understanding which study affords.

Other ways of favoring and nourishing personal devotion during the celebration of communal prayer include: allowing for some more-or-less lengthy periods of silence; pointing up the sacrificial character of the liturgy in which all Christians act as "priests" (not as actors but as vicars) of Jesus Christ himself, who is present among his people in prayer; building a real communion of faith and love among the people who pray together. The *last point* seems to be the most important, if the prayers recited together by a group of Christians (e.g., a religious community) are to be not only a public or liturgical celebration, but also a deeply-lived spiritual activity shared by all. Notwithstanding the same intention of praying together made by all, when there is an insufficient understanding or even a certain indifference among the members of a group, their choral utterance in prayer does not succeed in making a real community out of them. Thus, each one will feel more disturbed than helped, as far as his personal, inner prayer is concerned, by the words used by others in prayer. On the contrary, if the group is really one in mutual understanding and friendship, any formulas of vocal prayer can be helpful for confirming that already-existing deep communication of spirit. It is much like the experience people have when on a trip or a hike: people sing together whatever songs may come to mind to increase their team spirit.

Private-personal and public-communal prayers remain different and distinct in their patterns, methods and aims. Neither can be totally absorbed into the other. We need both, because we must be both individually involved in a deep life of prayer, and communally committed to giving corporate glory to God and encouragement to one another through our public prayers. Because of this duality, praying in both ways can be difficult at times. There may come the temptation to give up one form of prayer and rely on the other. There is also the temptation to view private and public prayer as if they were two parallel activities without any real connection with one another. The union between them in daily life requires effort on our part toward a synthesis in action.

Prayer as Experience

Another useful concept in describing prayer is the psychological viewpoint which is no less appropriate than "conversation" and "exercise." This is *"experience."* The prayerful *experience* of God is usually the effect of, or the result of the *exercise* of prayer. Prayer as an experience implies God's gifts and presence lavished on the praying person, who lovingly and consciously receives them. Today it seems that prayer is envisioned and approached more willingly as an experience than as an exercise, which we shall presently examine.

Preference for Experience

The "exercise" usually required by prayer is today almost obliterated. Notable evidence of this phenomenon is that methodical meditation does not have a "good press." Does this mean that all the exercises involved in prayer (i.e., silence, recollection, attention) are no longer relevant? Are they considered as merely boring and insignificant by contemporary man? While such "spiritual exercises" may be a necessary *predisposition* to prayer, they do seem to be only part of a previous ascetical training. Hence, they are not considered as specific elements of the properly "mystical" character of prayer, expressed by the idea of experience. If we look at recent "prayer movements" and ask the people involved in them what they think of their prayer life, they might describe it in terms of intimacy and ultimate experience. Their prayer appears predominantly as an intimate experience insofar as they neither pay much attention to, nor spend much time in any intellectual approach to God's presence. Indeed, they move directly toward a meeting with him.

Living in a too methodical, organized, and institutionaliz-
ed society, it seems that when they pray, they want to be
rid of all "techniques," methods, and rules for doing
things which stifle spontaneity and dissipate their zest.

Similarly, people seek and enjoy prayer as an ultimate
"peak-experience" because they are fed up or deeply
dissatisfied with the obsessive strivings of our society for
making money, achieving social status and success—
which are the typical aims of the work-ethic. These people
want to develop the spiritual dimensions of their
personalities, and their kinship with the eternal. After the
very extensive production of material and temporal
goods which has occurred in our industrial civilization,
people are now looking for values which are spiritual and
eternal, and which can be found only in God. In fact, and
notwithstanding the much-discussed secularization of
our modern world, our industrial, urban, technological
society has provoked in many persons a search for an
intimate and ultimate experience of God in prayer.

This divine experience is not at all envisioned as an
individualistic one. Christian prayer today is often an
experience enjoyed during communal celebrations. In
many prayer meetings (such as those organized by the
American charismatics, but also by other groups in
various nations) a prayerful experience of Christ's
mystery is discovered through more or less explicit
recollection of the Christ-event and the anticipation of his
coming in glory, lived in the awareness of Christ's
presence now through the Spirit. All of this is performed
in an atmosphere of festivity and creativity, of joyful
communion among those who are joined in the same faith
and love in the Spirit.

Contemporary man, overloaded by worldly
seriousness and the calculations of present-day society,
finds in prayer a new way of expressing his playful and

aesthetic spontaneity, an outlet for his artistic and poetical potentialities. Christians can enjoy the prayerful experience of their celebrations as a "recess from history-making, a time when they are not working, planning or recording. A time when they stop doing to simply be," as Harvey Cox puts it.

A moralistic religion is suspicious of any activity which appears to waste time, or, does not seem to serve the concrete interests of the commonwealth. But the praying Christian who celebrates with his brothers the dedication of his time, activity and attention to God alone, transcends the limits of a moralistic work-ethic. Such a Christian rightly believes that the whole of man is *not* in his history-making activity, but reaches the highest goal of his life when he can experience God's presence in prayer. Such experience is truly a foretaste of that contemplative love and adoration of the Holy Trinity which all the saints enjoy in eternal life.

On the other hand, definite risks are involved in this preference for prayer as experience. It is erroneous to say that we can reach an authentic and deep prayerful experience of God without going, at least swiftly, through the various acts proper to the discursive mind of man (reading, or meditating) and the required effective purifications of the heart. A prayer-experience resulting from a simplified approach to God's presence can easily be mixed with feelings and insights which lack depth, self-control and truth. It may also happen that if one lays too much stress on the experiential part of prayer, it becomes more difficult to overcome the temptation to discouragement when one has a difficult time in prayer—as when passing through a crisis of aridity. The only possibility of praying then is to resort to the traditional spiritual exercises and the spiritual efforts required by them.

Some Questions

A difficult problem concerning prayer as experience is whether and how the praying Christian *can* really experience God's presence. It seems that the prerequisites for such experience are:—on man's side: the actual and supernatural receptivity to the Holy Trinity given him by divinely infused grace and the theological virtues;—on the side of God: that magnificent gift of the Holy Trinity itself made to the sanctified Christian. Relying only on the super-human energies received by him through the divine infusion of grace and the theological virtues, a Christian can efficaciously assume that posture of receptive expectation which makes his experience of God possible. In the same way, it is only because God the Holy Trinity lavishes himself upon a Christian sanctified by grace and the theological virtues that the experiential enjoyment of the divine Persons is attainable. Actual Christian experience of the Trinity occurs only when the Holy Trinity dwelling within the human spirit meets there with the loving awareness of that same spirit, yearning with all faith, hope and charity (also prompted by the Holy Spirit) for the presence of the divine Persons.

This experience is the "mystical," i.e., silent and mysterious, character of Christian prayer. The reality in itself brings about an extremely rewarding experiential enjoyment of the Blessed Trinity. We are convinced that the praying Christian can experience the Holy Trinity because God grants this gift of himself. But the question of *how* such an experience (which is limited even after the infusion of grace and the theological virtues) can attain to God who is infinite, still remains unanswered. Does a Christian in and through prayer really "touch" the divine Persons? Or must he be content with the theological thrust which drives his spirit towards them, without however being able to "touch" them?

The typical darkness of faith certainly prevents the Christian from "seeing" the divine Persons. But how does he, then, "experience" them? Directly? Or, in the appeal they exercise on his loving awareness, as when a loving person in some way possesses in the very act of loving the attractive and moving "presence" of the beloved? Despite the knowledge we achieve through revelation and meditation, it is impossible to explain clearly just how the intimate meeting and union between a finite creature like man and the absolutely infinite being of God can occur. Therefore, the word "experience" means here not so much the fusion between the partners involved, as the *distinction* between them. There is an extremely clear-cut distinction in the case of a Christian who *experiences* the Holy Trinity in prayer.

Even though we do not know what the experience of prayer really implies from God's side, we can try to understand its impact on man. We cannot experience God in prayer without being, to some extent, saved or condemned by his Mercy and Majesty, Holiness and Justice, which are so vividly revealed to us when he comes, as it were, to "visit" us.

The tidying-up of the spirit and the purification of the heart are not perfectly accomplished when one meets and experiences God's splendor and sanctity in prayer. This is so true that when we first experience the presence of God, we feel equally confronted by an infinite holiness and sense ourselves to be judged by it. This is true because we become so vividly aware of our own sinfulness and impurity. "Leave me, Lord, for I am a sinner!" "It is terrible to fall into the hands of the living God!" This first manner of experiencing God's presence turns prayer into a confession of sins, a broken-hearted act of repentance, and an earnest desire to amend one's life. No real experience of God occurs in prayer unless such a sorrowful and painful feeling of unworthiness opens the way to it. An authentic religious experience of "The Sacred" necessarily involves the human perception of a "frightening mystery" (*mysterium tremendum*).

Together with that feeling of being judged and condemned, the experience of God in prayer is also sensed as *Salvation*: not eternal Salvation as if already fully received, but a real beginning of it as a "consoling mystery" (*mysterium fascinans*). When God comes to one of his faithful, he establishes a psychological presence of his Deity—which would be like something remaining outside of man's spirit and entering into him merely through its image. God also shares with the Christian his very *Being*! He enters personally into man's spirit and grants an ontological presence of himself. For this reason, we say that God sanctifies the Christian *in his very depths*, sharing with him his holiness, and offering to him his friendship.

It is not the experience of prayer which draws God into a Christian. God took the initiative in making himself present as Savior and Sanctifier, and he is always ready and willing to save and sanctify the whole person. By experiencing God's presence in prayer, the Christian opens himself up to receive the fullness of that saving and sanctifying power of God. In this respect, prayer can be defined as an action "assimilating God's personality and holiness into human life" (P.A. Liege, *What Is Christian Life*, Paramus: Paulist Press, 1964, p.71).

It is risky to over-emphasize the experiential character of prayer. The person praying might be tempted to stop at the human experience of devotion, without moving beyond it into the mystery of God. Some modern thinkers, who speak much about the human experience of the transcendent, do not really want to go into all the metapaphysical implications of it. In their opinion, prayer is a psychological-existential experience devoid of an objective ontological content. In this case, prayer is reduced to a subjective experience of the *state of the human spirit*. It is not truly an experience of God. Such subjective experience becomes merely "secularized prayer."

In Conclusion

Our foregoing considerations have developed both a theological and a psychological approach to prayer. All of our progress has been "situated" on the side of God's presence and human awareness of him. This is the mountainside of the spirit where the sun shines.

We have spoken of prayer as the descent of God from heaven to meet us and our ascent to welcome him into our hearts. In analyzing the main elements and moments of this intimate encounter, we had many opportunities to unfold the extent of the biblical revelation of God's presence—as well as to explore its theological depths. In addition, the complexity of the responsive awareness of man before God was clarified by pointing out the psychological dialectics of prayer as exercise and prayer as experience, both of which merge into the conversation of prayer.

Journeying through a little-known land we have become more aware of the loving kindness of our God, who offers us his companionship in a wonderful experience of light and joy found in his presence. We have seen that the core of prayer (as with God's presence itself, of which prayer is the awareness), is beyond any vocal, discursive or emotive human exercise. In fact, too many mental images can flood the inner awareness of God; too much talking can jam God's personal revelation and the human spirit's response to him; too many feelings can obscure the pure light of God. True prayer thrives in the depths of man's spirit, beyond all words, emotions or thoughts which may at various times surface in human awareness. True prayer is an innermost awareness which remains after the passing of all internal and external expressions of prayer. This is the only prayer which permits us to "pray always without ceasing" as Jesus asks of us. The intellectual journey we have made through the previous pages was grounded upon this deep core of prayer, and we have endeavored to achieve a systematic theological reflection. A random collection of insights on prayer, beautiful and inspiring as they might be, could scarcely convince the mind, and would not help a Christian very much toward leading a fully conscious and creative prayer life.

The concept of "loving awareness of God's presence" has played an enlightening role in helping us to understand prayer. But certainly it is not fully adequate for manifesting the whole mystery of prayer. It gives in a nutshell a clear description of the first dawning of contemplative prayer in the human spirit, but it does not say anything about that zone of darkness which expands over a long stretch in the journey of prayer; one which covers the highest mountains of contemplation. In fact, the climbers of those heights tell us of an unexpected overturning of God's luminous presence into a staggering, obscure experience of his absence. Instead of the enjoyable awareness of a present God, the praying Christian now experiences the painful yearning for a God who seems to absent himself, after having dwelt as a most beloved Guest within the human soul. Such a Christian— apparently deprived of God's presence—cannot help but strive with burning desire for him who seems to flee away. Accordingly, another long stretch in the journey of prayer begins from the moment God withdraws his luminous presence from the praying Christian's awareness. Prayer now becomes a journey through a thick cloud of darkness, during which a purifying faith is the only guide and support of the soul.

To try to understand the reason for such an abrupt "about-face" on God's part toward his dearest friends would require a biblico-theological study of God's mysterious "wholly-otherness" or transcendence. To trace the itinerary of this most extraordinary path in the human journey through prayer would demand at least as many pages as we have here dedicated to the loving awareness of his presence.

SELECTED BIBLIOGRAPHY

Baelz, P.R.   *Prayer and Providence,* London: Chapman, 1968.

Bloom, A.   *Living Prayer,* London: Darton, Longman & Todd, 1966.

——   *Beginning to Pray,* Paramus: Paulist Press, 1970.

——   *God and Man,* Paramus: Newman-Paulist Press, 1971. Ch. IV: "Holiness and Prayer," a conference given in Louvain, 1969.

— and Lefevre, G. *Courage to Pray,* London: Darton, Longman & Todd, 1973.

Boase, L.   *The Prayer of Faith,* London: Darton, Longman & Todd, 1975.

Borrows, R.   *Outline of Mystical Prayer,* London: Sheed & Ward, 1976. Fundamental teaching on prayer of the Carmelite masters.

Boyd, M.   *Are You Running with Me, Jesus?,* New York: Holt, Rinehart and Winston, 1966. Prayer is not so much talking to God as just sharing his presence.

Boylan, M.E. *Difficulties in Mental Prayer,* West-

5

4

minster: Newman Press, 1965. Solutions to difficulties in mental prayer.

Bro, B.　*Learning to Pray,* Staten Island: Alba House, 1966. A general treatise on prayer, dealing also with mental prayer.

Carroll, J.　*Prayer from Where You Are,* Dayton: G. Pflaum, Witness Books, 1970.

——　*A Terrible Beauty,* Paramus: Paulist-Newman, 1973.

Carthusian　*The Prayer of Love and Silence,* Denville, Dimension Books, 1962. A short introduction to the spiritual life.

Catherine of Siena　*The Dialogue,* Rockford: TAN Books, 1974. A treatise on prayer, pp. 158-280.

Congar, Y.　*The Mystery of the Temple,* Paramus: Newman Press, 1958. Biblical teaching of the presence of God.

Colin, L.　*The Meaning of Prayer,* Westminster: Newman, 1962.

Corbishley, T.　*The Prayer of Jesus,* London: Oxford, 1976.

Doyle, C.H.　*The Nature and Methods of Mental Prayer,* Huntington: Our Sunday Visitor Press. Excellent for older children.

Dubay, T.　*God Dwells in Us,* Denville: Dimension Books, 1971.

——　*Pilgrims Pray,* Staten Island: Alba House, 1976. A simple discussion of the prayer themes found in both testaments.

Farrell, E.J.　*Prayer Is a Hunger,* Denville: Dimension Books, 1972. An un-systematic spiritual reflection on prayer.

——　*Surprised by the Spirit,* Denville: Dimension Books, 1973. Prayerful meditations

Godin, A., ed. *From Cry to Word: Studies in the Psychology of Religion,* Brussels: Lumen Vitae, 1967.

Guillerand, A. *The Prayer of the Presence of God,* Denville: Dimension Books, 1966.

Hakenwerth, Q. *The Prayer of Faith,* St. Louis: Maryhurst Press, 1966. Prayer is the encounter with God within us.

Hamman, A. *Prayer: The New Testament,* Chicago: Franciscan Herald Press, 1971.

Haring, B. *Prayer, the Integration of Faith and Life,* London: St. Paul Publications, 1975.

Higgins, J.J. *Thomas Merton on Prayer,* Garden City: Doubleday and Co., 1973.

Hinnebusch, P. *Praise, A Way of Life,* Ann Arbor: Word of Life Publications, 1976.

Hocken, P. *Prayer, a Gift of Life,* Paramus: Paulist Press, 1974. The communal character of prayer, enlivened by the Spirit.

Hoffman, D. *The Life Within,* New York: Sheed & Ward, 1966.

Lefevre, G. *Simplicity, The Heart of Prayer,* Paramus: Paulist Press, 1975.

Lewis, C.S. *Letters to Malcolm: Chiefly on Prayer,* London: Geoffrey Bles, 1964.

Lotz, J.B. *Interior Prayer: The Exercise of Personality,* New York: Herder & Herder, 1968.

Maloney, G.A. *Stillness,* Denville: Dimension Books, 1976.

Maritain, J. *Liturgy and Contemplation,* London: Geoffrey Chapman, 1960.

Martin, F. *Touching God,* Denville: Dimension Books, 1975.

Martin, R. *Hungry for God,* Garden City: Doubleday and Co., 1974.

Merton, T.   *A Balanced Life of Prayer,* Abbey of
               Gethsemani: Trappist Press, 1951.
——   *Contemplative Prayer,* Garden City:
               Doubleday and Co., Image Books, 1971.
——   *No Man Is an Island,* Garden City:
               Doubleday and Co., Image Books, 1976.
——   *Spiritual Direction and Meditation,*
               Collegeville: Liturgical Press, 1959.
Moschner, F.M. *Christian Prayer,* St. Louis: Herder
               Book Co., 1962.
Nedocelle, M. *Christian Prayer,* St. Louis: Herder
               Book Co., 1962.
Nouwen, J.M.H. *Reaching Out: The Three Movements
               of the Spiritual Life,* Garden City: Double-
               day and Co., 1975.
——   *With Open Hands,* Notre Dame: Ave
               Maria Press, 1972. In words and pictures, a
               view of prayer that relates to the central
               experience of life.
Phillips, D.Z. *The Concept of Prayer,* London: Geoffrey
               Chapman, 1965.
Pieper, J.   *Happiness and Contemplation,* Chicago:
               Henry Regnery Co., 1966.
Quiery, W.   *Facing God,* New York: Sheed & Ward,
               1967.
Quoist, M.   *Prayer,* New York: Sheed & Ward, 1963.
Raguin, Y.   *How To Pray: A Book of Spiritual
               Reflections,* Wheathampstead: A. Clark,
               1973.
Rahner, K.   *On Prayer,* New York: Deus Books, 1968.
St. Teresa of Avila   Her works are available in the
               Image book series.
Slade, H.   *Exploration into Contemplative Prayer,*
               London: Darton, Longman & Todd, 1975.
Sheets, J.   *The Spirit in Us: Personal Prayer in the*

New Testament, Denville: Dimension Books, 1969.

Stanley, D.M. *Boasting in the Lord: the Phenomenon of Prayer in St. Paul,* Paramus: Paulist Press, 1973.

Trueman Dicken, E.W. *The Crucible of Love: A Study of the Mysticism of St. Teresa of Jesus and of St. John of the Cross,* New York: Sheed & Ward, 1963.

Tugwell, S. *Prayer. Vol. I: Living with God; Vol. II: Prayer in Practice,* Dublin: Veritas Publications, 1974.

van Zeller, H. *Approach to Prayer,* New York: Guild Press, 1966. Deals also with mental prayer. Good for beginners.

von Balthasar, H.U. *Prayer,* New York: Deus Books, 1961. A theological treatise on prayer and contemplation, for advanced readers.

Whelan, J.P. *Benjamin: Essays on Prayer,* Paramus: Paulist Press, 1972